The NYSTROM
ATLAS *of* OUR COUNTRY

FALCON HEIGHTS ELEMENTARY SCHOOL
1393 W. GARDEN AVE.
FALCON HTS, MN 55113

NYSTROM
DIVISION OF HERFF JONES, INC.

Educational Consultant: Barbara Winston
Northeastern Illinois University
Chicago, Illinois

Picture credits appear inside the back cover.

For information about ordering this atlas, call toll-free 800-621-8086.

2000 Edition

Copyright © 1996 NYSTROM Division of Herff Jones, Inc.
3333 Elston Avenue, Chicago, Illinois 60618

10 9 8 7   01 00

ISBN: 0-7825-0589-9   Product Code Number: 9A91

Printed in U.S.A.

CONTENTS

The Nystrom Atlas of Our Country includes a variety of maps—political, physical, regional, and thematic. Photographs, art of various kinds, and graphs appear throughout the book. The section that deals with the history of the United States also makes use of illustrated time frames. Each kind of map and pictorial display is best suited to certain purposes.

Political Maps

Political maps in this atlas are colored by state or by country. The colors make it as easy as possible to tell where one place ends and another begins. Names of capitals and other major cities can be found quickly because the maps are edited to keep them uncluttered.

Physical Maps

Physical maps in this atlas are designed so that the names and relative locations of natural features can be seen at a glance. On the maps of the world and the United States, the land colors stand for different elevations above sea level. Countries, states, and selected cities also are named.

Regional Maps

Regional maps in this atlas offer close-up views of areas on the political map of the United States. Because regional maps enlarge the areas shown, they can name more cities while remaining easy to read. The regional maps also include the names of many land and water features.

Thematic Maps

Thematic maps focus on single subjects or themes. One type in this atlas is a simple kind of physical map that names large natural regions. Another type focuses on historical events. Others map patterns of rainfall, climate, population, land use, natural vegetation, and other special themes.

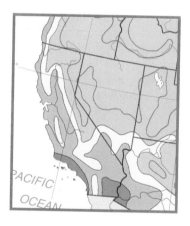

Time Frames

Time frames appear across the bottom of every pair of facing pages in the history section. The events shown on the upper part of the pages occurred within the time frame's outer dates. The time frame provides a historical setting by illustrating other significant events of the period.

Tables and Graphs

Tables are compact, orderly arrangements of facts. Graphs summarize facts in a visual way, making it easier to see comparisons and trends. Circle graphs, for example, show how parts add up to a whole. Other kinds of graphs in this atlas help you picture change over time.

Photographs and Art

Photographs can show natural settings or record events like nothing else can. Maps are entirely symbolic. The realism of photographs helps bring map symbolism to life. Art can serve the same purpose when photographs are not available. It is especially useful for illustrating history maps.

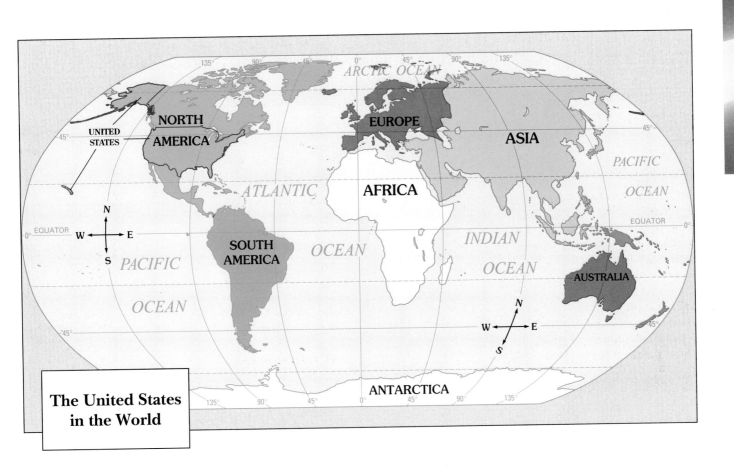

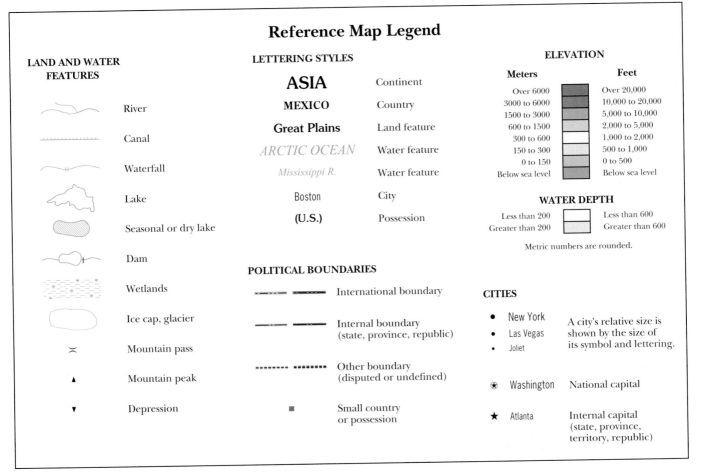

Reference Map Legend

LAND AND WATER FEATURES

	River
	Canal
	Waterfall
	Lake
	Seasonal or dry lake
	Dam
	Wetlands
	Ice cap, glacier
≍	Mountain pass
▲	Mountain peak
▼	Depression

LETTERING STYLES

ASIA	Continent
MEXICO	Country
Great Plains	Land feature
ARCTIC OCEAN	Water feature
Mississippi R.	Water feature
Boston	City
(U.S.)	Possession

POLITICAL BOUNDARIES

	International boundary
	Internal boundary (state, province, republic)
	Other boundary (disputed or undefined)
▪	Small country or possession

ELEVATION

Meters		Feet
Over 6000		Over 20,000
3000 to 6000		10,000 to 20,000
1500 to 3000		5,000 to 10,000
600 to 1500		2,000 to 5,000
300 to 600		1,000 to 2,000
150 to 300		500 to 1,000
0 to 150		0 to 500
Below sea level		Below sea level

WATER DEPTH

Less than 200		Less than 600
Greater than 200		Greater than 600

Metric numbers are rounded.

CITIES

●	New York	A city's relative size is shown by the size of its symbol and lettering.
●	Las Vegas	
●	Joliet	
⊛	Washington	National capital
★	Atlanta	Internal capital (state, province, territory, republic)

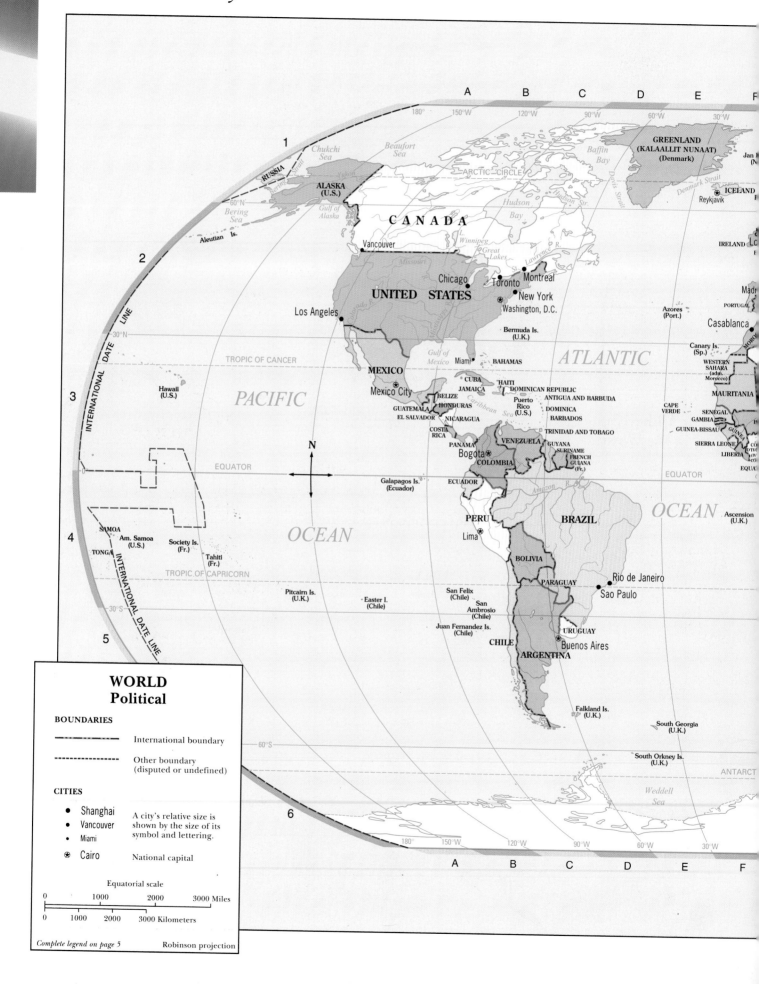

WORLD
Political

BOUNDARIES

— · — · — International boundary

- - - - - - Other boundary
(disputed or undefined)

CITIES

● Shanghai   A city's relative size is
● Vancouver shown by the size of its
• Miami   symbol and lettering.

⊛ Cairo   National capital

Equatorial scale

0   1000   2000   3000 Miles

0 1000 2000 3000 Kilometers

Complete legend on page 5   Robinson projection

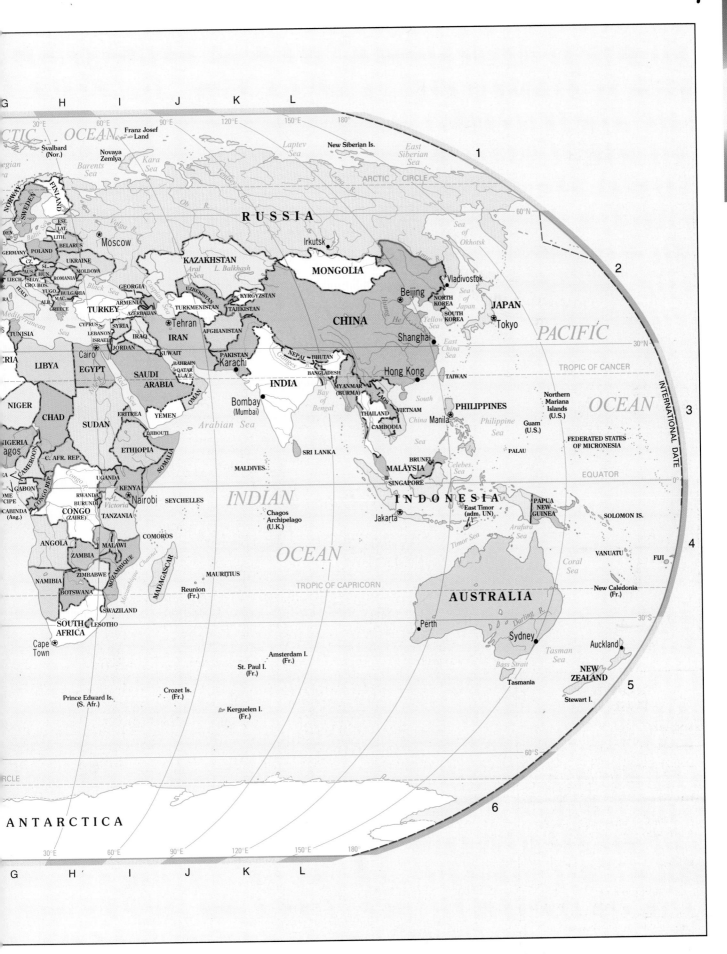

ARCTIC OCEAN

30°E 60°E 90°E 120°E 150°E 180°

Svalbard (Nor.)

Franz Josef Land

Novaya Zemlya

Laptev Sea

New Siberian Is.

East Siberian Sea

1

Barents Sea

Kara Sea

ARCTIC CIRCLE

NORWAY SWEDEN FINLAND

RUSSIA

60°N

EST. LAT. LITH.

Moscow

Irkutsk

Sea of Okhotsk

2

GERMANY POLAND BELARUS

Volga R.

Amur R.

CZ. UKRAINE

KAZAKHSTAN

Ob R.

MONGOLIA

Vladivostok

Sea of Japan

AUS. HUN. MOLDOVA

Aral Sea

L. Balkhash

LIECH. SLOV. ROMANIA

Beijing

NORTH KOREA

JAPAN

CRO. BOS. BULGARIA

Black Sea

GEORGIA

UZBEKISTAN

KYRGYZSTAN

CHINA

Huang He

SOUTH KOREA

Tokyo

PACIFIC

ITALY YUGO. MAC.

ARMENIA

TURKMENISTAN

TAJIKISTAN

ALB. GREECE

TURKEY

AZERBAIJAN

Shanghai

East China Sea

30°N

Mediterranean Sea

CYPRUS

Tehran

AFGHANISTAN

TROPIC OF CANCER

TUNISIA

LEBANON SYRIA

IRAQ

IRAN

NEPAL BHUTAN

Hong Kong

TAIWAN

ISRAEL JORDAN KUWAIT

PAKISTAN

Ganges

BANGLADESH

Cairo

BAHRAIN QATAR

Karachi

INDIA

MYANMAR (BURMA)

Northern Mariana Islands (U.S.)

OCEAN

3

LIBYA EGYPT

SAUDI

U.A.E.

LAOS

NIGER

ARABIA

OMAN

Bombay (Mumbai)

Bay of Bengal

THAILAND

VIETNAM

PHILIPPINES

Manila

Guam (U.S.)

CHAD SUDAN

ERITREA

YEMEN

Arabian Sea

CAMBODIA

South China Sea

Philippine Sea

FEDERATED STATES OF MICRONESIA

NIGERIA Lagos

DJIBOUTI

ETHIOPIA

SRI LANKA

PALAU

CAMEROON

SOMALIA

MALDIVES

BRUNEI

Celebes Sea

SÃO TOMÉ PRÍNCIPE

GABON

C. AFR. REP.

UGANDA

MALAYSIA

CABINDA (Ang.)

CONGO REP.

RWANDA

KENYA

SINGAPORE

EQUATOR

0°

CONGO (ZAIRE)

BURUNDI

L. Victoria

Nairobi

SEYCHELLES

Chagos Archipelago (U.K.)

INDONESIA

East Timor (adm. UN)

PAPUA NEW GUINEA

SOLOMON IS.

TANZANIA

Jakarta

Arafura Sea

ANGOLA

MALAWI

COMOROS

INDIAN

4

ZAMBIA

MOZAMBIQUE

MADAGASCAR

Mozambique Channel

OCEAN

Coral Sea

VANUATU

FIJI

NAMIBIA

ZIMBABWE

BOTSWANA

MAURITIUS

Reunion (Fr.)

TROPIC OF CAPRICORN

AUSTRALIA

New Caledonia (Fr.)

30°S

SWAZILAND

SOUTH AFRICA

LESOTHO

Amsterdam I. (Fr.)

Perth

Darling R.

Cape Town

St. Paul I. (Fr.)

Sydney

Auckland

Tasman Sea

Bass Strait

NEW ZEALAND

5

Prince Edward Is. (S. Afr.)

Crozet Is. (Fr.)

Kerguelen I. (Fr.)

Tasmania

Stewart I.

60°S

CIRCLE

6

ANTARCTICA

30°E 60°E 90°E 120°E 150°E 180°

G H I J K L

INTERNATIONAL DATE

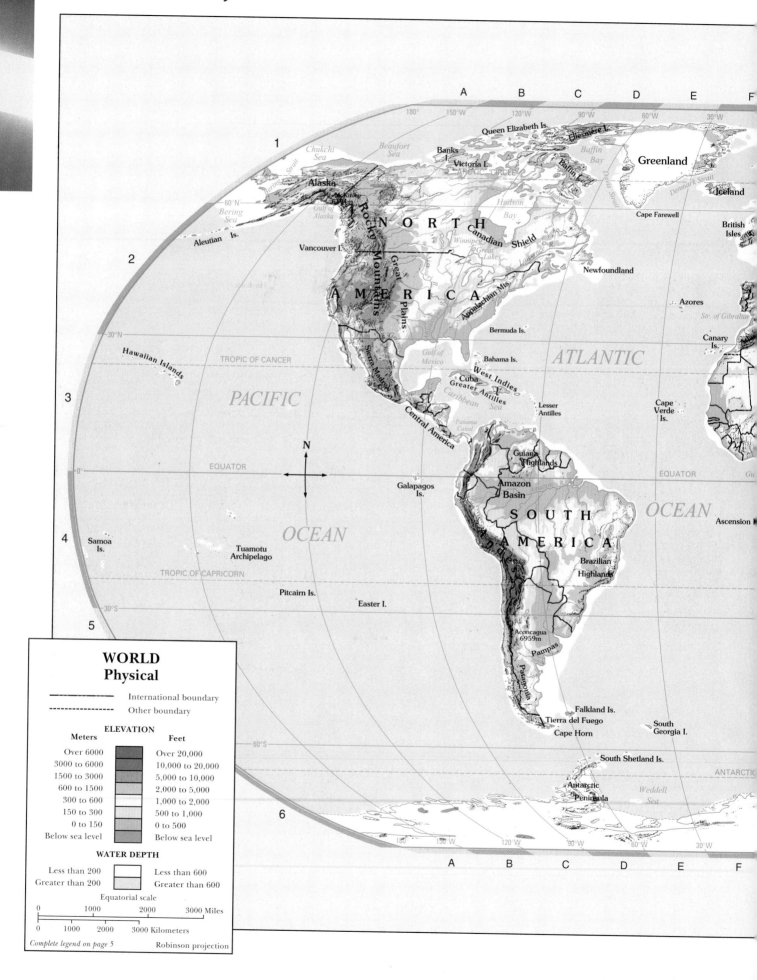

Complete legend on page 5

WORLD
Physical

——————— International boundary

- - - - - - - - Other boundary

ELEVATION

Meters		Feet
Over 6000		Over 20,000
3000 to 6000		10,000 to 20,000
1500 to 3000		5,000 to 10,000
600 to 1500		2,000 to 5,000
300 to 600		1,000 to 2,000
150 to 300		500 to 1,000
0 to 150		0 to 500
Below sea level		Below sea level

WATER DEPTH

Less than 200		Less than 600
Greater than 200		Greater than 600

Equatorial scale

0   1000   2000   3000 Miles

0   1000   2000   3000 Kilometers

Robinson projection

G   H   I   J   K   L

OCEAN

30°E   60°E   90°E   120°E   150°E   180°

Svalbard
Novaya
Zemlya
North Cape
Kara
Sea
Barents
Sea
Severnaya
Zemlya
Laptev
Sea
New Siberian
Is.
East
Siberian
Sea

1

Scandinavia
Central
Siberian
Plateau
West
Siberian
Plain
Ob. R.
Siberia
East
Siberian
Uplands
Kolyma Range
60°N

Northern
European
Plain
Ural Mountains
A S I A
Lena R.
Kamchatka
Peninsula
Sea
of
Okhotsk

EUROPE
Steppes
L. Balkhash
Altai Mts.
Gobi
(Desert)
Manchurian
Plain
Sakhalin

2

Caucasus
Mt. Elbrus
5642m
Black Sea
Caspian Sea
Tien Shan
Kunlun Mts.
Plateau of Tibet
North
China
Plain
Hokkaido
Sea
of
Japan
Honshu

Sicily
Mediterranean
Sea
Plateau
of Iran
Hindu Kush
Himalayas
8850m
Yunnan
Plateau
Yellow
Sea
Kyushu
Ryukyu Is.
East
China
Sea
PACIFIC

30°N

Sahara
Hoggar
Mts.
Tibesti
Mts.
Arabian
Peninsula
Persian Gulf
Deccan
Plateau
Bay
of
Bengal
Indochina
Peninsula
Taiwan
TROPIC OF CANCER

AFRICA
Sahel
Arabian Sea
Sri
Lanka
South
China
Sea
Philippine
Is.
Mariana
Is.
OCEAN

3

Ethiopian
Highlands
Maldives
Philippine
Sea
Guam
Caroline Is.
Marshall
Is.

Congo Basin
Congo R.
Mt. Kilimanjaro
5895m
Celebes
Sea
Borneo
Celebes
EQUATOR

0°

INDIAN
Seychelles
Chagos
Archipelago
Sumatra
New Guinea
Solomon Is.

Bie
Plateau
Comoros
Java
Timor
Arafura
Sea

Mauritius
OCEAN
Timor Sea
Coral
Sea
Fiji Is.

4

Kalahari
Desert
Madagascar
Mozambique Channel
TROPIC OF CAPRICORN
Great Sandy
Desert
Great Barrier Reef
New
Caledonia

Drakensberg
Amsterdam I.
AUSTRALIA
Great Dividing Range

Cape of Good Hope
St. Paul I.
Cape Leeuwin
Great Victorian
Desert
Darling R.
Mt. Kosciuszko
2228m
Tasman
Sea
30°S

Kerguelen I.
Bass Strait
Tasmania
New
Zealand

5

60°S

ARCTIC CIRCLE

6

ANTARCTICA

30°E   60°E   90°E   120°E   150°E   180

G   H   I   J   K   L

Origin and Spread of Native Americans

→ Spread of early inhabitants
▭ Present coastline
▭ Ice Age coastline
— U.S. boundaries today

Orthographic projection

Mammoths roamed the earth during the last Ice Age. Hunters may have followed such game across the Bering land bridge and stayed to become America's first inhabitants.

Native American Population, 1492

Estimated inhabitants

Per 100 sq. km	Per 100 sq. miles
None	None
0 to 1	0 to 3
1 to 8	3 to 20
8 to 40	20 to 100
40 to 150	100 to 400
Over 150	Over 400

The Great Serpent Mound in southern Ohio is about 1/4 mile long. It was built about 700 B.C. by the Adena, one of several Indian cultures who were mound builders.

20,000 B.C.
Cro-Magnon artists decorate caves in Europe during the last Ice Age.

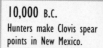

10,000 B.C.
Hunters make Clovis spear points in New Mexico.

2600 B.C.
The Great Pyramid is built in Egypt.

People of the mound-builder culture fashioned many beautiful objects. This figure of a bird is cut from copper and inlaid with a mother-of-pearl eye.

The Maya and Aztecs built palaces and pyramid-like temples a thousand years before Columbus. But by the time the Spanish arrived, the Maya civilization had been weakened by warfare.

Native American and European Populations in 1492

Estimated population

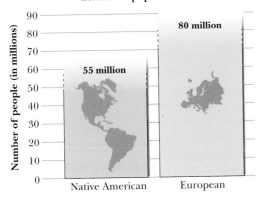

55 million — Native American
80 million — European

Number of people (in millions)

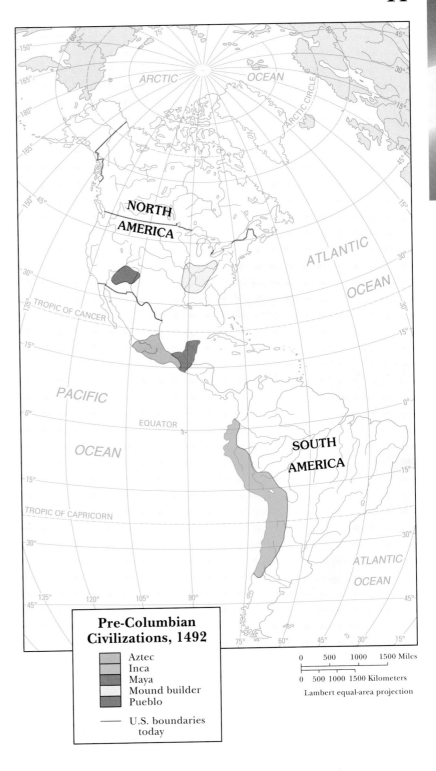

NORTH AMERICA
SOUTH AMERICA
ATLANTIC OCEAN
PACIFIC OCEAN
ARCTIC OCEAN
TROPIC OF CANCER
EQUATOR
TROPIC OF CAPRICORN

Pre-Columbian Civilizations, 1492

- Aztec
- Inca
- Maya
- Mound builder
- Pueblo
- — U.S. boundaries today

0 500 1000 1500 Miles
0 500 1000 1500 Kilometers
Lambert equal-area projection

44 B.C. Julius Caesar is crowned Dictator of Rome.

1454 Johann Gutenberg's printing press makes books more available.

1492

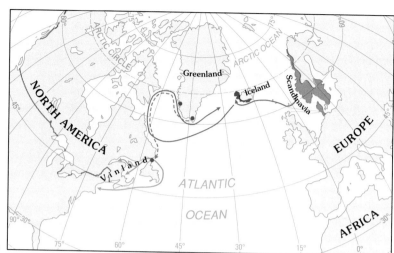

Viking Voyages to Greenland and Vinland

- Scandinavia
- → Herjolfsson, 985
- ⇢ Ericson, 1000
- → Other Norse voyages (unconfirmed), 1000–1020
- • Norse settlement
- — U.S. boundaries today

Orthographic projection

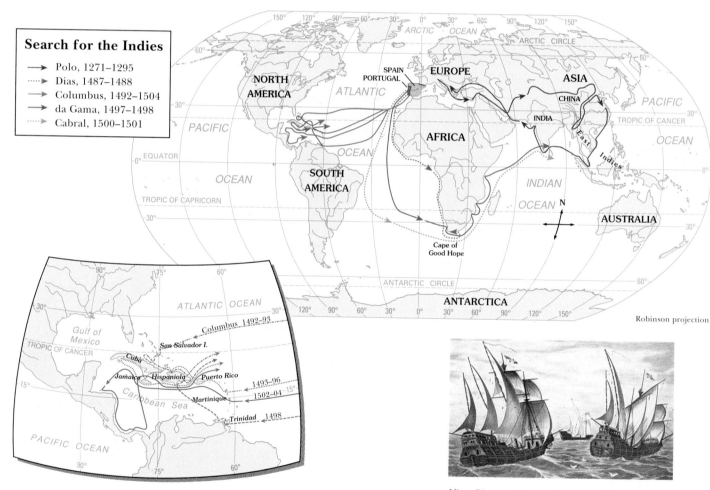

Search for the Indies

- → Polo, 1271–1295
- ⇢ Dias, 1487–1488
- → Columbus, 1492–1504
- → da Gama, 1497–1498
- ⇢ Cabral, 1500–1501

Robinson projection

Nina, Pinta, and *Santa Maria* were the ships used by Columbus on his quest for the Indies. He had a crew of 90.

985
Vikings cross the Atlantic Ocean and settle in Greenland.

1096–1270
European armies invade Asia in a series of Crusades.

900

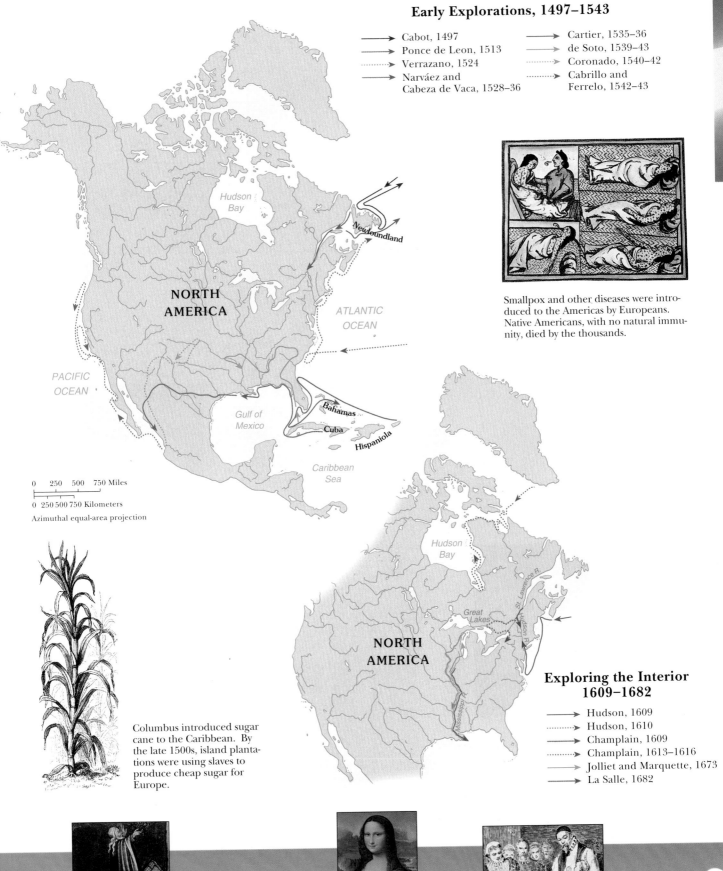

Early Explorations, 1497–1543

→ Cabot, 1497
→ Ponce de Leon, 1513
⋯⋯> Verrazano, 1524
→ Narváez and
   Cabeza de Vaca, 1528–36

→ Cartier, 1535–36
→ de Soto, 1539–43
⋯⋯> Coronado, 1540–42
⋯⋯> Cabrillo and
   Ferrelo, 1542–43

Hudson Bay

Newfoundland

NORTH AMERICA

ATLANTIC OCEAN

PACIFIC OCEAN

Gulf of Mexico

Bahamas

Cuba

Hispaniola

Caribbean Sea

```
0    250  500   750 Miles
0  250 500 750 Kilometers
```
Azimuthal equal-area projection

Smallpox and other diseases were introduced to the Americas by Europeans.
Native Americans, with no natural immu-
nity, died by the thousands.

Columbus introduced sugar
cane to the Caribbean. By
the late 1500s, island planta-
tions were using slaves to
produce cheap sugar for
Europe.

Hudson Bay

Great Lakes

St. Lawrence R.

Hudson R.

NORTH AMERICA

Mississippi R.

Exploring the Interior
1609–1682

→ Hudson, 1609
⋯⋯> Hudson, 1610
→ Champlain, 1609
⋯⋯> Champlain, 1613–1616
→ Jolliet and Marquette, 1673
→ La Salle, 1682

1347–1351
The plague known as the Black Death
kills 25,000,000 Europeans.

1503
The *Mona Lisa* is painted
by Leonardo da Vinci.

1587
Virginia Dare is the first
English child born in America.

1682

Colonial North America, 1640

- British
- Dutch
- French
- Spanish
- Swedish
- Not claimed

Boston, 1630   Date founded

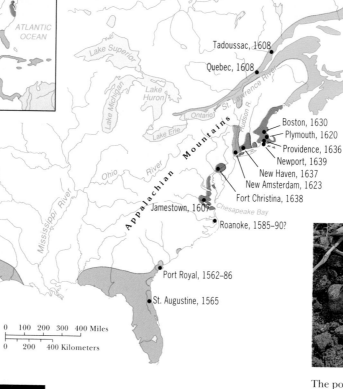

Tadoussac, 1608
Quebec, 1608
Boston, 1630
Plymouth, 1620
Providence, 1636
Newport, 1639
New Haven, 1637
New Amsterdam, 1623
Fort Christina, 1638
Jamestown, 1607
Roanoke, 1585–90?
Port Royal, 1562–86
St. Augustine, 1565

ARCTIC OCEAN
ATLANTIC OCEAN
PACIFIC OCEAN

Lake Superior
Lake Michigan
Lake Huron
Lake Erie
Lake Ontario
St. Lawrence River
Hudson R.
Appalachian Mountains
Ohio River
Mississippi River
Chesapeake Bay

0   100   200   300   400 Miles
0   200   400 Kilometers

The potato was native to the Andes Mountains and was cultivated by the Inca. By 1625 it had become the key food crop in Ireland.

Tobacco was smoked in pipes by American Indians long before the voyages of Columbus. Colonists in Virginia grew tobacco and exported it to England by the early 1600s.

Marquette   Joliet   Dubuque

French explorers, mapmakers, traders, and settlers were the first Europeans in many parts of North America. Their influence is seen in many place names, including the three above and those below:

Des Moines	Louisiana	St. Louis
Baton Rouge	New Orleans	Sault Ste. Marie
Fond du Lac	La Crosse	Terre Haute

1492

1599
Shakespeare's plays are performed at the Globe Theater in London.

1620
The Pilgrims land at Plymouth on Massachusetts Bay.

1638
Swedish settlers build the first log cabins in America.

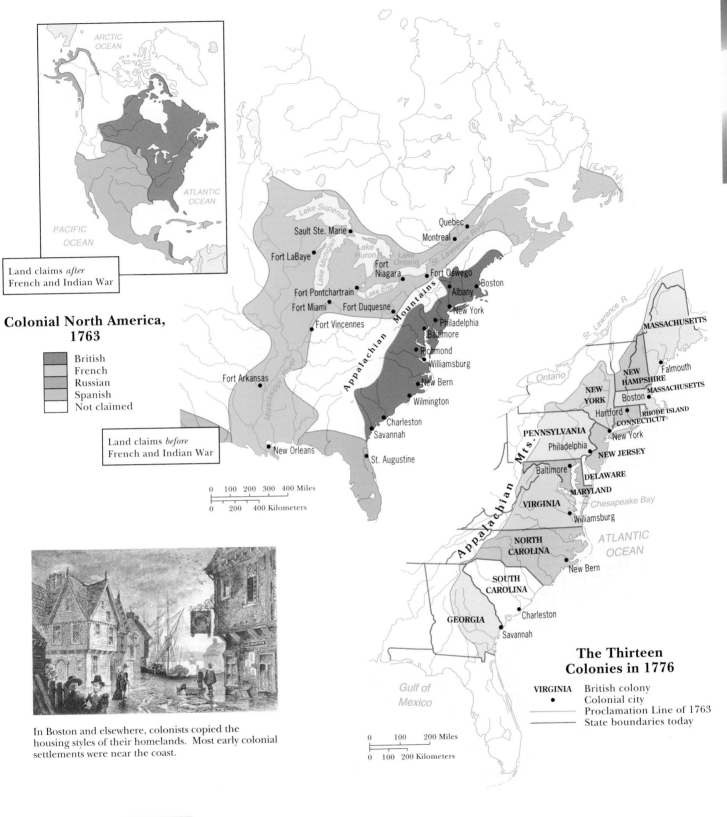

ARCTIC OCEAN

ATLANTIC OCEAN

PACIFIC OCEAN

Land claims *after* French and Indian War

Colonial North America, 1763

British
French
Russian
Spanish
Not claimed

Land claims *before* French and Indian War

Lake Superior
Sault Ste. Marie
Fort LaBaye
Lake Michigan
Lake Huron
Fort Niagara
Fort Pontchartrain
Lake Erie
Lake Ontario
Fort Miami
Fort Duquesne
Fort Vincennes
Fort Arkansas
Mississippi River
New Orleans

Quebec
Montreal
St. Lawrence River
Fort Oswego
Boston
Albany
New York
Appalachian Mountains
Philadelphia
Baltimore
Richmond
Williamsburg
New Bern
Wilmington
Charleston
Savannah
St. Augustine

0 100 200 300 400 Miles
0 200 400 Kilometers

The Thirteen Colonies in 1776

St. Lawrence R.
L. Ontario
MASSACHUSETTS
NEW HAMPSHIRE
Falmouth
NEW YORK
Boston
MASSACHUSETTS
Hartford
RHODE ISLAND
CONNECTICUT
PENNSYLVANIA
New York
Philadelphia
NEW JERSEY
Baltimore
DELAWARE
Appalachian Mts.
MARYLAND
Chesapeake Bay
VIRGINIA
Williamsburg
ATLANTIC OCEAN
NORTH CAROLINA
New Bern
SOUTH CAROLINA
Charleston
GEORGIA
Savannah
Gulf of Mexico

VIRGINIA   British colony
•   Colonial city
Proclamation Line of 1763
State boundaries today

0 100 200 Miles
0 100 200 Kilometers

In Boston and elsewhere, colonists copied the housing styles of their homelands. Most early colonial settlements were near the coast.

1670
The Hudson's Bay Company begins trading for furs in North America.

1754–1763
The English Colonies fight the French and Indian War.

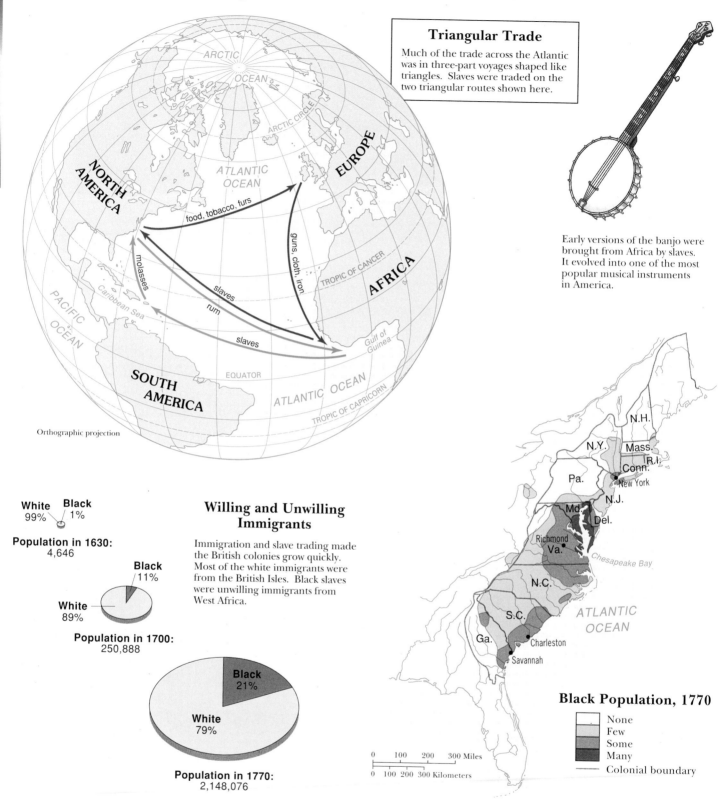

Orthographic projection

Triangular Trade

Much of the trade across the Atlantic was in three-part voyages shaped like triangles. Slaves were traded on the two triangular routes shown here.

Early versions of the banjo were brought from Africa by slaves. It evolved into one of the most popular musical instruments in America.

Willing and Unwilling Immigrants

Immigration and slave trading made the British colonies grow quickly. Most of the white immigrants were from the British Isles. Black slaves were unwilling immigrants from West Africa.

White 99% Black 1%
Population in 1630: 4,646

Black 11%
White 89%
Population in 1700: 250,888

Black 21%
White 79%
Population in 1770: 2,148,076

Black Population, 1770

- None
- Few
- Some
- Many
- Colonial boundary

0 100 200 300 Miles
0 100 200 300 Kilometers

1500s
The Songhai Empire dominates West African trade and culture.

1614
Pocahontas, daughter of an Indian chief, marries Englishman John Rolfe.

1619
African slaves are brought into Virginia for the first time.

1492

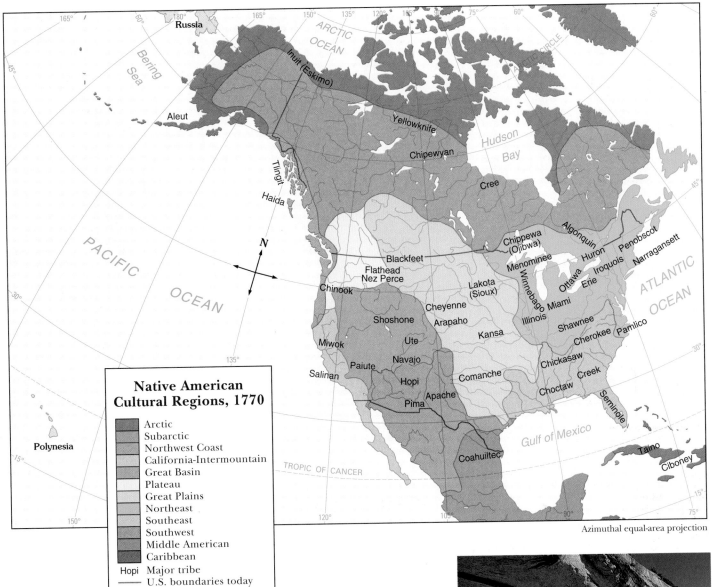

Native American Cultural Regions, 1770

- Arctic
- Subarctic
- Northwest Coast
- California-Intermountain
- Great Basin
- Plateau
- Great Plains
- Northeast
- Southeast
- Southwest
- Middle American
- Caribbean

Hopi   Major tribe
——   U.S. boundaries today

Azimuthal equal-area projection

Before Columbus, the horse was unknown to American Indians. But they were riding the descendants of escaped Spanish horses by the early 1600s.

The Anasazi built the cliff dwellings at Mesa Verde around 1200. The largest, shown here, has about 200 rooms and parts that are four stories high.

1692
Witchcraft trials begin in Salem, Massachusetts.

1775
Paul Revere warns that the British redcoats are coming.

1776

Santa Barbara was the site of one of the missions built by the Spanish in California between 1769 and 1823. The missions were religious outposts of the Roman Catholic Church.

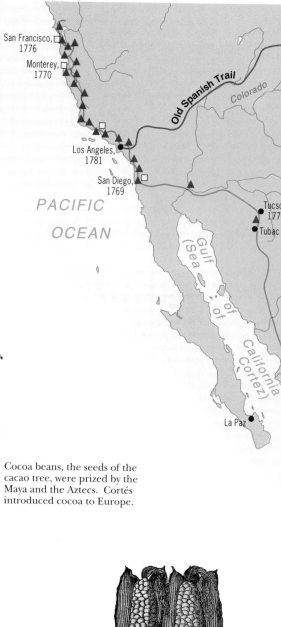

San Francisco, 1776

Monterey, 1770

Old Spanish Trail

Colorado

Los Angeles, 1781

San Diego, 1769

PACIFIC OCEAN

Tucson 1776

Tubac

Gulf of California (Sea of Cortez)

La Paz

NORTH AMERICA

Cocoa beans, the seeds of the cacao tree, were prized by the Maya and the Aztecs. Cortés introduced cocoa to Europe.

Spain in the Americas, 1500s

Spanish explorers

→ Balboa, 1513
·····▸ Cortés, 1519
→ Pizarro, 1532
→ Coronado, 1540–42

• Large Spanish settlement
▨ Extent of Spanish influence

SOUTH AMERICA

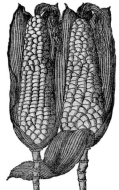

Corn was grown by Indians from Canada to Argentina. It was unknown elsewhere until Columbus returned to Spain with corn seed.

1492

1532
The gold of the Inca draws Spanish conquerors to Peru.

1547
Ivan the Terrible becomes the first czar of all Russia.

1588
The Spanish Armada is defeated by English warships.

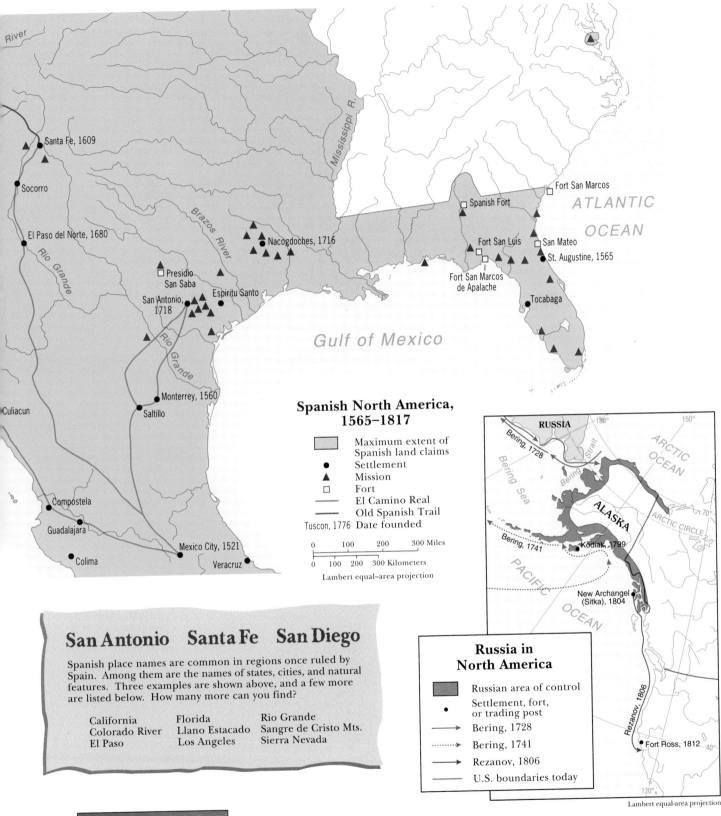

Spanish North America, 1565–1817

- ☐ (shaded) Maximum extent of Spanish land claims
- ● Settlement
- ▲ Mission
- ☐ Fort
- —— El Camino Real
- —— Old Spanish Trail
- Tuscon, 1776 Date founded

0 100 200 300 Miles
0 100 200 300 Kilometers
Lambert equal-area projection

Santa Fe, 1609
Socorro
El Paso del Norte, 1680
Río Grande
Presidio San Saba
San Antonio, 1718
Espiritu Santo
Nacogdoches, 1716
Brazos River
Spanish Fort
Fort San Marcos
ATLANTIC OCEAN
Fort San Luis
San Mateo
St. Augustine, 1565
Fort San Marcos de Apalache
Tocabaga
Gulf of Mexico
Mississippi R.
Monterrey, 1560
Saltillo
Culiacun
Compostela
Guadalajara
Colima
Mexico City, 1521
Veracruz

San Antonio Santa Fe San Diego

Spanish place names are common in regions once ruled by Spain. Among them are the names of states, cities, and natural features. Three examples are shown above, and a few more are listed below. How many more can you find?

California	Florida	Rio Grande
Colorado River	Llano Estacado	Sangre de Cristo Mts.
El Paso	Los Angeles	Sierra Nevada

Russia in North America

- ▨ Russian area of control
- ● Settlement, fort, or trading post
- → Bering, 1728
- ⋯→ Bering, 1741
- → Rezanov, 1806
- —— U.S. boundaries today

RUSSIA
Bering, 1728
Bering Strait
ARCTIC OCEAN
Bering Sea
ALASKA
ARCTIC CIRCLE
Bering, 1741
Kodiak, 1799
New Archangel (Sitka), 1804
PACIFIC OCEAN
Rezanov, 1806
Fort Ross, 1812

Lambert equal-area projection

1653
The Taj Mahal is built in India.

1769
Father Junipero Serra founds Mission San Diego.

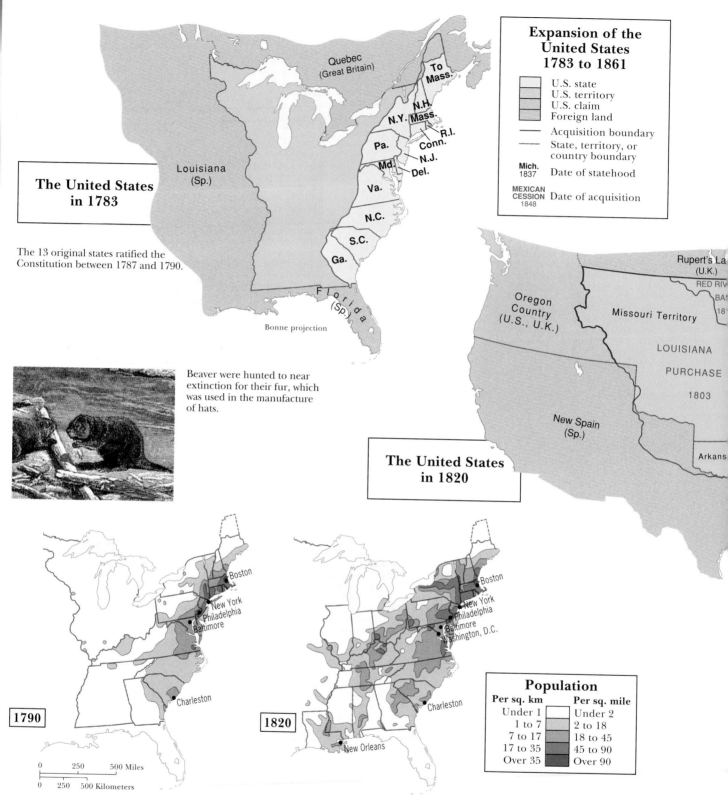

Expansion of the
United States
1783 to 1861

- U.S. state
- U.S. territory
- U.S. claim
- Foreign land
— Acquisition boundary
— State, territory, or country boundary

Mich.
1837 Date of statehood

MEXICAN
CESSION Date of acquisition
1848

Quebec
(Great Britain)

To
Mass.

N.H.
N.Y. Mass.
R.I.
Pa. Conn.
N.J.
Md. Del.
Va.

N.C.

S.C.

Ga.

Florida
(Sp.)

Louisiana
(Sp.)

The United States
in 1783

The 13 original states ratified the
Constitution between 1787 and 1790.

Bonne projection

Beaver were hunted to near
extinction for their fur, which
was used in the manufacture
of hats.

Rupert's La
(U.K.)
RED RIV
BAS
18

Oregon
Country
(U.S., U.K.)

Missouri Territory

LOUISIANA

PURCHASE

1803

New Spain
(Sp.)

Arkans

The United States
in 1820

Boston
New York
Philadelphia
Baltimore

Charleston

1790

Boston
New York
Philadelphia
Baltimore
Washington, D.C.

Charleston

New Orleans

1820

Population

Per sq. km	Per sq. mile
Under 1	Under 2
1 to 7	2 to 18
7 to 17	18 to 45
17 to 35	45 to 90
Over 35	Over 90

0   250   500 Miles

0   250   500 Kilometers

1776
The Declaration of Independence
is signed.

1789–1797
George Washington
serves as the 1st
President.

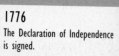

1776

Gold was discovered in California in 1848 and "gold fever" swept the country. Thousands of prospectors traveled west to seek their fortunes.

After Texas declared its independence in 1836, Mexican troops stormed the Alamo. The 200 defenders of the fort were killed, and "Remember the Alamo!" became an American war slogan.

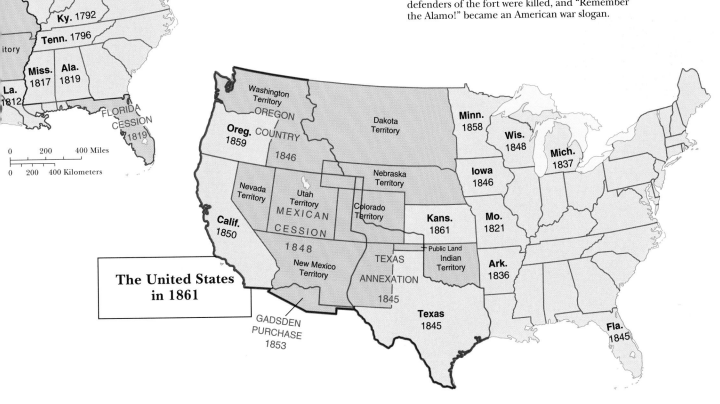

Lower Canada (U.K.)

Upper Canada (U.K.)

Maine 1820

Vermont 1791

Michigan Territory

Ill. 1818 **Ind.** 1816 **Ohio** 1803

Ky. 1792

Tenn. 1796

itory

Miss. 1817 **Ala.** 1819

La. 1812

FLORIDA CESSION 1819

0   200   400 Miles

0   200   400 Kilometers

Washington Territory

OREGON

Oreg. 1859   COUNTRY   1846

Dakota Territory

Minn. 1858

Wis. 1848

Mich. 1837

Nevada Territory

Utah Territory   MEXICAN

Nebraska Territory

Iowa 1846

Calif. 1850

CESSION 1848

Colorado Territory

Kans. 1861

Mo. 1821

New Mexico Territory

TEXAS

Public Land Indian Territory

Ark. 1836

The United States in 1861

ANNEXATION 1845

GADSDEN PURCHASE 1853

Texas 1845

Fla. 1845

1793 Eli Whitney's cotton gin makes cotton a profitable crop.

1814 Francis Scott Key writes "The Star-Spangled Banner."

1835 Samuel Colt invents the revolver.

1861

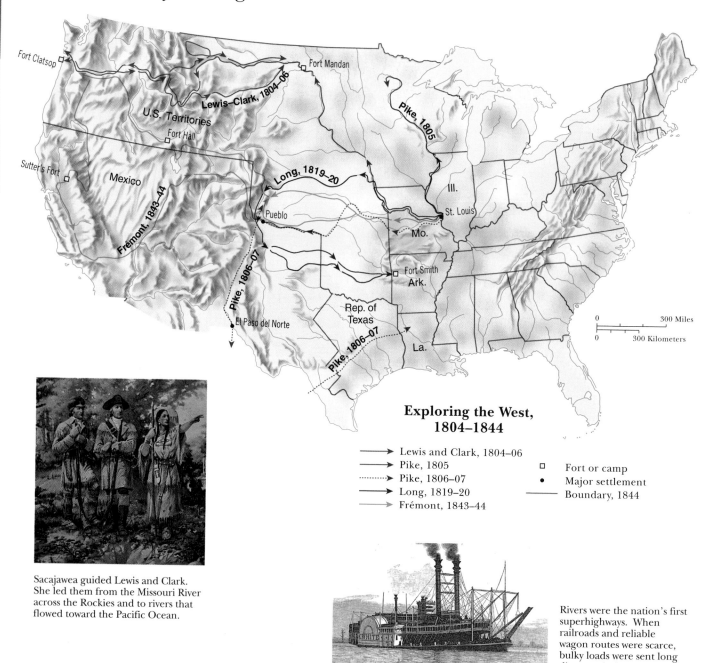

Exploring the West, 1804–1844

⟶ Lewis and Clark, 1804–06
⟶ Pike, 1805
⟶ Pike, 1806–07
⟶ Long, 1819–20
⟶ Frémont, 1843–44

□ Fort or camp
● Major settlement
— Boundary, 1844

Sacajawea guided Lewis and Clark. She led them from the Missouri River across the Rockies and to rivers that flowed toward the Pacific Ocean.

Rivers were the nation's first superhighways. When railroads and reliable wagon routes were scarce, bulky loads were sent long distances by boat.

Cross Section of the United States

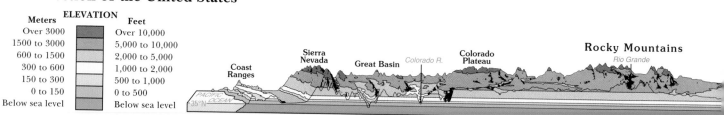

Meters	ELEVATION	Feet
Over 3000		Over 10,000
1500 to 3000		5,000 to 10,000
600 to 1500		2,000 to 5,000
300 to 600		1,000 to 2,000
150 to 300		500 to 1,000
0 to 150		0 to 500
Below sea level		Below sea level

1776

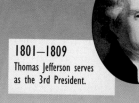

1781
The War of Independence ends.

1801–1809
Thomas Jefferson serves as the 3rd President.

1825
The Erie Canal helps link the East with the West.

Few pioneers made the long journey west alone. Most joined other families for protection and formed long wagon trains.

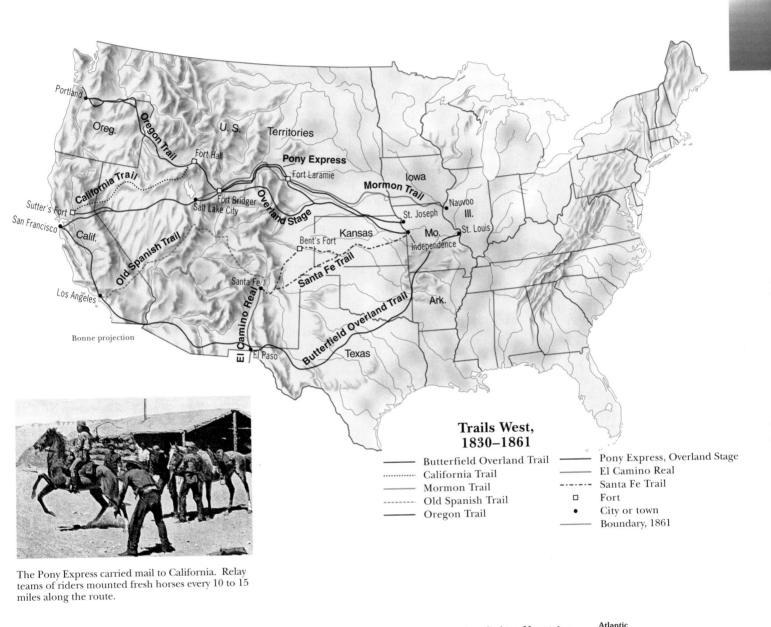

Trails West, 1830–1861

- —— Butterfield Overland Trail
- ·········· California Trail
- —— Mormon Trail
- – – – Old Spanish Trail
- —— Oregon Trail
- —— Pony Express, Overland Stage
- —— El Camino Real
- –·–·– Santa Fe Trail
- □ Fort
- ● City or town
- —— Boundary, 1861

Bonne projection

The Pony Express carried mail to California. Relay teams of riders mounted fresh horses every 10 to 15 miles along the route.

Great Plains   **Ozark Plateau**   Mississippi R.   Tennessee R.   **Central Lowland**   **Appalachian Mountains**   **Atlantic Coastal Plain**

ATLANTIC OCEAN

35°N

1830
"Tom Thumb" is the first steam locomotive to pull passengers.

1861
The telegraph connects the West Coast with the East Coast.

1861

The Second Wave of Immigration, 1820–1890

As in the past, most newcomers in the mid-1800s were from Northern and Western Europe. But more and more came from countries besides Great Britain. Irish, German, and Scandinavian immigrants were changing the country's ethnic make-up. (Africans sold into slavery were not counted as voluntary immigrants.)

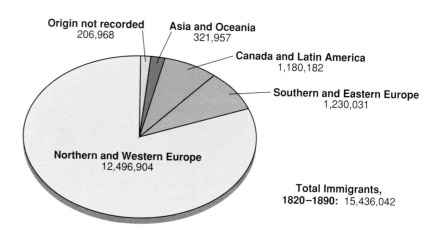

Origin not recorded
206,968

Asia and Oceania
321,957

Canada and Latin America
1,180,182

Southern and Eastern Europe
1,230,031

Northern and Western Europe
12,496,904

Total Immigrants,
1820–1890: 15,436,042

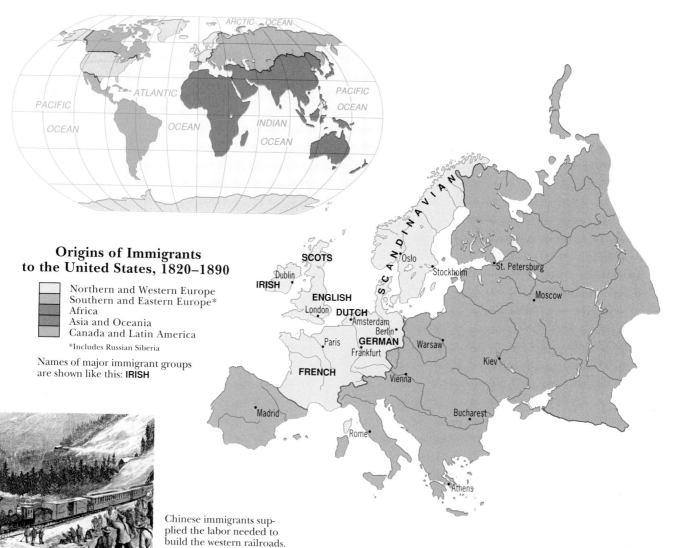

Origins of Immigrants to the United States, 1820–1890

Northern and Western Europe
Southern and Eastern Europe*
Africa
Asia and Oceania
Canada and Latin America

*Includes Russian Siberia

Names of major immigrant groups are shown like this: **IRISH**

Chinese immigrants supplied the labor needed to build the western railroads. Many settled in California.

1829–1837
Andrew Jackson serves as the 7th President.

1845–1854
Irish farmers face starvation when their potato crops fail.

Thousands of immigrants entered New York and other cities every year. Newcomers often worked at low-paying jobs and lived in crowded slums.

The government forced the eastern Indians to migrate west of the Mississippi River, to the new Indian Territory. The Cherokee called their journey the Trail of Tears.

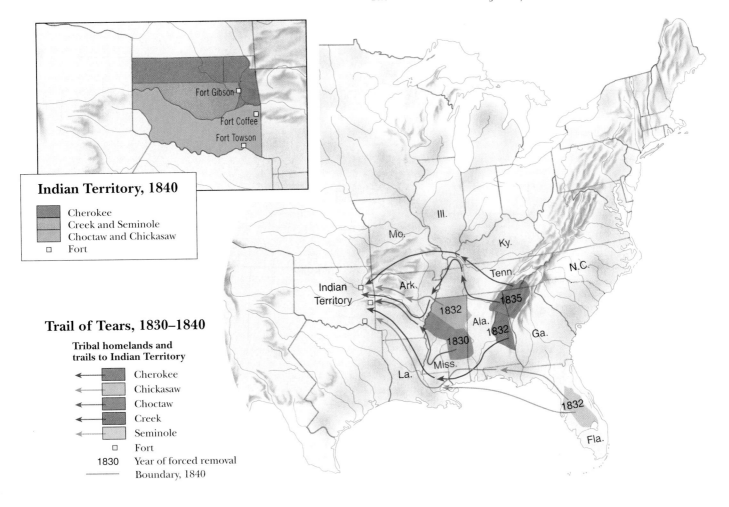

Indian Territory, 1840

- Cherokee
- Creek and Seminole
- Choctaw and Chickasaw
- □ Fort

Trail of Tears, 1830–1840

Tribal homelands and trails to Indian Territory

- Cherokee
- Chickasaw
- Choctaw
- Creek
- Seminole
- □ Fort
- 1830 Year of forced removal
- Boundary, 1840

1876
Custer dies at the Battle of the Little Bighorn in Montana.

1880
Canned fruits and vegetables appear on store shelves.

1886
The Statue of Liberty is placed in New York Harbor.

1890

Textile mills in the Northeast mechanized the manufacture of cloth and changed the way of work. Young women and even children began working in factories.

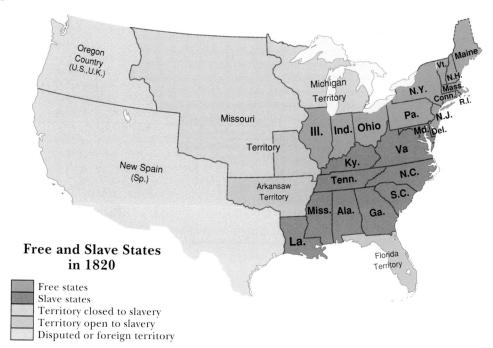

Free and Slave States in 1820

Free states
Slave states
Territory closed to slavery
Territory open to slavery
Disputed or foreign territory

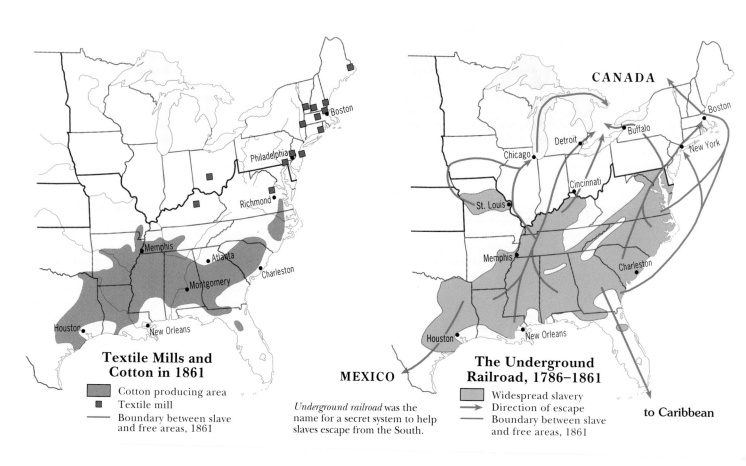

Textile Mills and Cotton in 1861

Cotton producing area
■ Textile mill
— Boundary between slave and free areas, 1861

Underground railroad was the name for a secret system to help slaves escape from the South.

The Underground Railroad, 1786–1861

Widespread slavery
→ Direction of escape
— Boundary between slave and free areas, 1861

1831
Nat Turner leads a slave revolt in Virginia.

1837
John Deere invents a steel plow that will cut tough prairie sod.

Free and Slave States in 1861

Free states
Slave states
Territory open to slavery

The Civil War was fought in large part over slavery. It lasted from 1861 to 1865 and was by far the bloodiest American war. When it was over, slavery was outlawed.

The South was far less industrialized than the North. Its economy depended on plantation farming, which in turn depended on slavery. The South's main crop was "King Cotton."

Free and Slave States in 1861

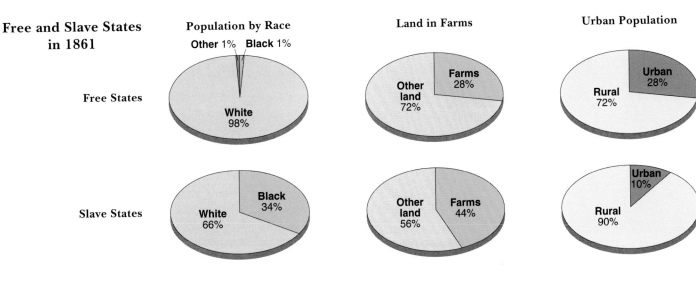

Population by Race

Free States
- Other 1%
- Black 1%
- White 98%

Slave States
- Black 34%
- White 66%

Land in Farms

Free States
- Farms 28%
- Other land 72%

Slave States
- Other land 56%
- Farms 44%

Urban Population

Free States
- Urban 28%
- Rural 72%

Slave States
- Urban 10%
- Rural 90%

1852
The novel *Uncle Tom's Cabin* helps spread anti-slavery sentiment.

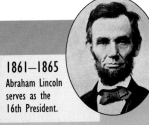

1861–1865
Abraham Lincoln serves as the 16th President.

1879
Thomas Alva Edison invents the electric light bulb.

1890

Cattle Trails and Railroads, 1861–1900

☐ Great Plains cattle region, 1880

→ Chisholm Trail
→ Goodnight-Loving Trail
→ Sedalia Trail
→ Western Trail

·········· Major railroad line
● Town at trailhead
● Other railroad stop
—— Boundary, 1900

Cattle drives in the West brought large herds to the railroads for shipment to markets in the East.

Population

Per sq. km	Per sq. mile
Under 1	Under 2
1 to 7	2 to 18
7 to 17	18 to 45
17 to 35	45 to 90
Over 35	Over 90

1861

1900

1861
The Apache begin forty years of warfare against the U.S.

1872
Yellowstone becomes the first National Park.

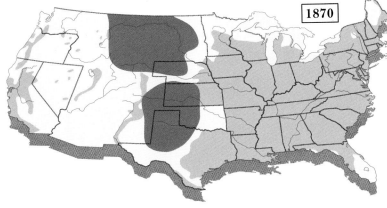
1870

Decline of Buffalo, Growth of Agriculture

Range of buffalo
Agriculture and other productive land use

At the end of the Civil War, there were about 15 million buffalo on the Great Plains. They were soon split into northern and southern herds by the railroad. The railroad also brought hunters, both professional and amateur. By 1889 fewer than 600 buffalo remained.

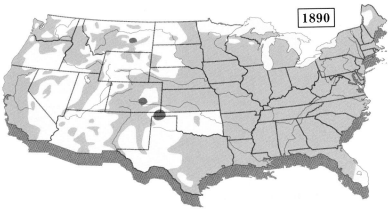
1890

At Promontory, Utah, in 1869, the Central Pacific and Union Pacific lines met. They formed the first railroad to connect the East and West.

Barbed wire fenced farmland on the treeless western plains. The first farmhouses were built with blocks of sod, the tough topsoil held together by matted roots.

Reduced Travel Times

Fastest times from New York to San Francisco

.... Before 1861: boat, railroad, stagecoach, 35 days

– – – 1861: railroad and stagecoach, 26 days

——— 1869: transcontinental railroad, 7 days

0   300 Miles

0   300 Kilometers

1876
Alexander Graham Bell invents the telephone.

1880s
Hunters destroy the last big herds of buffalo.

1900
Once numbering millions, the last passenger pigeons are killed.

1900

The Third Wave of Immigration, 1890–1929

In the 1890s and early 1900s, a vast flood of peoples poured into the United States. Unlike in the past, most of the newcomers were from Southern and Eastern Europe. They had a major impact on the size and ethnic character of our cities.

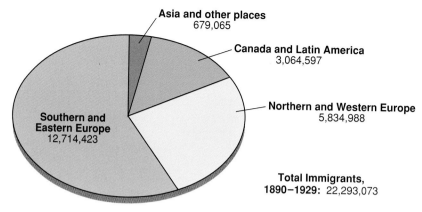

Asia and other places
679,065

Canada and Latin America
3,064,597

Northern and Western Europe
5,834,988

Southern and Eastern Europe
12,714,423

Total Immigrants,
1890–1929: 22,293,073

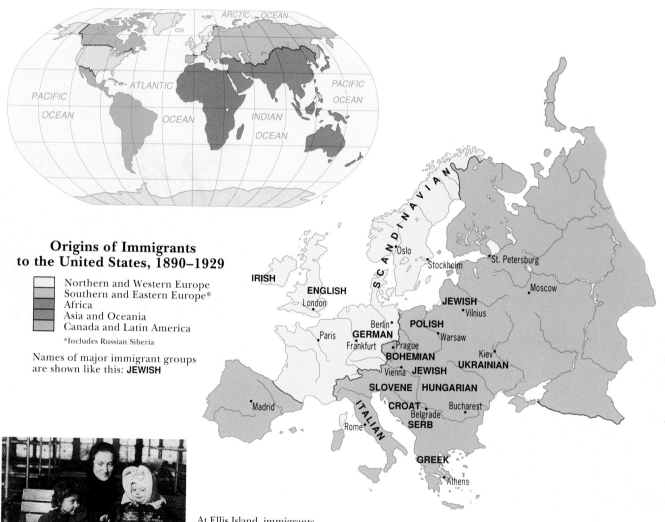

Origins of Immigrants to the United States, 1890–1929

Northern and Western Europe
Southern and Eastern Europe*
Africa
Asia and Oceania
Canada and Latin America
*Includes Russian Siberia

Names of major immigrant groups are shown like this: **JEWISH**

At Ellis Island, immigrants waited their turn to be examined by doctors and questioned by officials. Few were turned away.

1892
Ellis Island opens as an immigrant receiving station.

1908
Ford Motor Company introduces the Model T.

1890

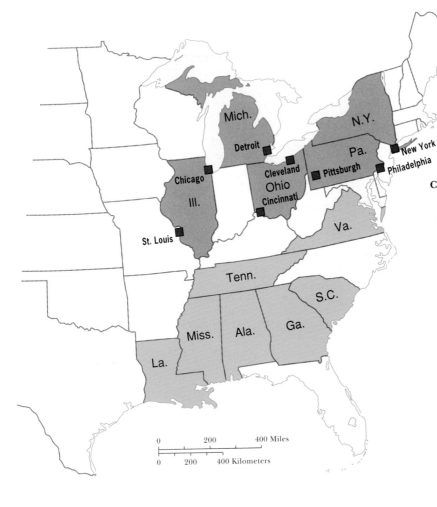

Black Migration to Northern Cities During World War I

Change due to black migration, 1910–1920

■ City—large gain from migration

State—large gain from migration

State—large loss to migration

Labor shortages caused by World War I attracted many African Americans to jobs in the North.

0   200   400 Miles

0   200   400 Kilometers

African Americans kept moving to Northern cities through the 1920s. They sought to escape the bitter race relations and poverty of the rural South.

Shiploads of immigrants entered the United States after a stop at Ellis Island in New York Harbor.

Urban and Rural Populations in 1920

Rural 49% 51,552,647

Urban 51% 54,157,973

1914
The Panama Canal connects the Atlantic and Pacific Oceans.

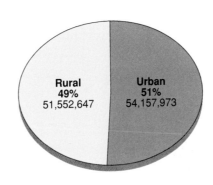

1917–1918
U.S. troops fight in World War I.

1920s
Radios bring entertainment to the home.

1929

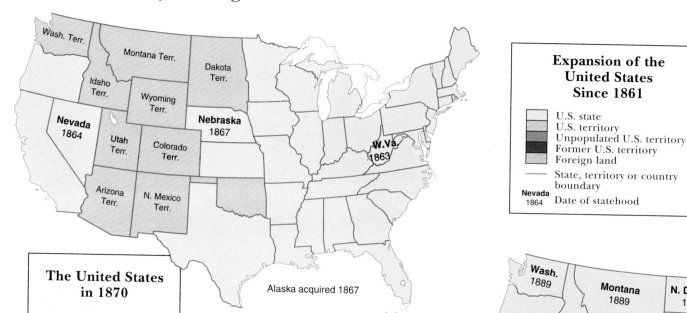

**The United States
in 1870**

Alaska acquired 1867

**Expansion of the
United States
Since 1861**

U.S. state
U.S. territory
Unpopulated U.S. territory
Former U.S. territory
Foreign land
——— State, territory or country
boundary
**Nevada
1864** Date of statehood

Shawnee Dakota Huron

The Indian names for rivers, lakes, and other features often
were borrowed by the settlers who came later. Several states
are named after Indian tribes, and others have the Indian
names of rivers that flow through them. Here are just a few
of the many other Indian names still in use:

Allegheny   Ouachita   Tacoma
Kalamazoo   Sheboygan   Tallahassee
Oshkosh   Shenandoah Yosemite

**Wash.
1889**   **Montana
1889**   **N. Dakota
1889**

**Idaho
1890**   **Wyoming
1890**   **S. Dakota
1889**

**Utah
1896**   **Colorado
1876**

**Arizona
1912**   **New
Mexico
1912**   **Okla
1907**

**The United States
in 1912**

Native American Lands Today

▰ Large reservation
· Other reservation or community

The reservations shown are areas set
aside by the government for use by
American Indians. Almost half of the
1,800,000 Indians in the United States
live on reservations.

1884
The first steel-frame skyscraper
is built in Chicago.

1901–1909
Theodore Roosevelt serves
as the 26th President.

1903
The Wright brothers fly their first
airplane at Kitty Hawk, N.C.

The Indian Territory in Oklahoma was opened to white settlers in the late 1800s. At the official opening of a choice section, thousands rushed to claim the best sites.

Ethnic Diversity in Hawaii, 1959

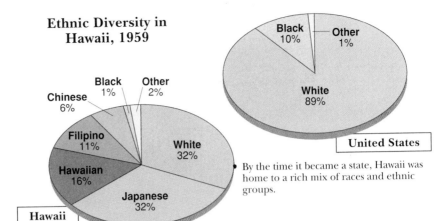

Hawaii
- Chinese 6%
- Black 1%
- Other 2%
- White 32%
- Japanese 32%
- Hawaiian 16%
- Filipino 11%

United States
- Black 10%
- Other 1%
- White 89%

By the time it became a state, Hawaii was home to a rich mix of races and ethnic groups.

Theodore Roosevelt led the Rough Riders in the Spanish-American war of 1898. The United States won and took control of Guam, the Philippines, and Puerto Rico.

Hawaii acquired 1898

0   200   400 Miles

0   200   400 Kilometers

The United States Today

1898 Date acquired as territory

0   1000   2000 Miles

0   1000   2000 Kilometers

Modified oblique orthographic projection

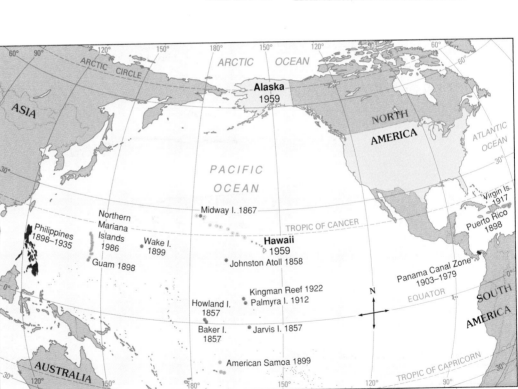

ARCTIC CIRCLE

ARCTIC OCEAN

Alaska 1959

ASIA

NORTH AMERICA

ATLANTIC OCEAN

PACIFIC OCEAN

Midway I. 1867

TROPIC OF CANCER

Virgin Is. 1917

Puerto Rico 1898

Northern Mariana Islands 1986

Wake I. 1899

Hawaii 1959

Johnston Atoll 1858

Philippines 1898–1935

Guam 1898

Kingman Reef 1922

Panama Canal Zone 1903–1979

Howland I. 1857

Palmyra I. 1912

EQUATOR

SOUTH AMERICA

N

Baker I. 1857

Jarvis I. 1857

American Samoa 1899

AUSTRALIA

TROPIC OF CAPRICORN

1920
Women gain the constitutional right to vote.

1950s
Televisions become common in homes.

Now

The Dust Bowl, 1932–1936

Topsoil blown away by wind

- Severe loss
- Moderate loss

Dust storms drove 350,000 people from their farms during the Great Depression. Many families migrated as far as California in search of work.

(Map labels: Mont., N. Dak., Minn., Wyo., S. Dak., Nebr., Iowa, Colo., Kans., N. Mex., Okla., Texas)

Years of drought on the Great Plains led to huge dust storms. Tons of topsoil were blown from an area known as the Dust Bowl.

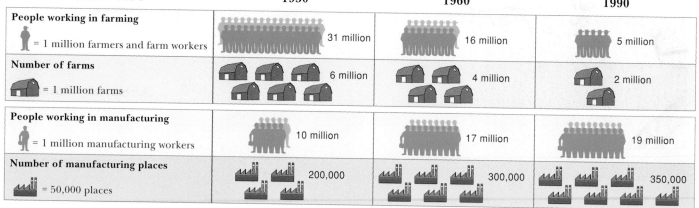

(Map labels: Calif., Oakland, Los Angeles, Texas, Dallas, Houston, Wis., Mich., Detroit, Chicago, Ill., Ind., Cleveland, Ohio, Ky., Ark., Tenn., Miss., Ala., Ga., La., Fla., N.C., S.C., Va., W.V., Penn., N.Y., Newark, New York, Philadelphia, N.J., Md., Baltimore, Washington, D.C., Conn.)

The Great Migration, 1940–1970

Change due to black migration

- City—large gain from migration
- State—large gain from migration
- State—large loss to migration

During the Great Migration, 5 million blacks moved from the South. It was one of the largest mass movements in human history.

Farming and Manufacturing, 1930–1990

	1930	1960	1990
People working in farming = 1 million farmers and farm workers	31 million	16 million	5 million
Number of farms = 1 million farms	6 million	4 million	2 million
People working in manufacturing = 1 million manufacturing workers	10 million	17 million	19 million
Number of manufacturing places = 50,000 places	200,000	300,000	350,000

1929 The Great Depression begins, putting millions out of work.

1933–1945 Franklin D. Roosevelt serves as the 32nd President.

1941–1945 U.S. troops fight in World War II.

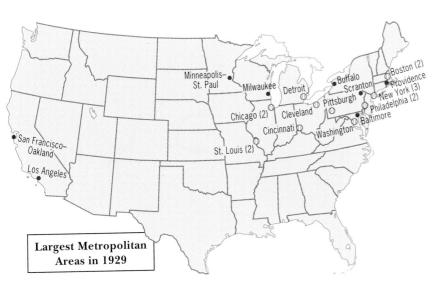

Largest Metropolitan Areas in 1929

Willie Mays began his major league career in 1951 with the New York Giants. In 1958 the brilliant center fielder moved with his team to San Francisco.

Major League Expansion and the Growth of Cities, 1929–1994

Cleveland Ⓣ Major league baseball site

Portland ● Other large metropolitan area

(2) Number of teams in area

In 1929 there were 16 major league baseball teams. Most were in the large metropolitan areas of the Northeast. By 1994 the U.S. had 26 major league teams. Most of the new and relocated teams were in the South and West.

Largest Metropolitan Areas in 1994

Children wait for their friends after getting polio shots, a common experience in the 1950s. African Americans were changing the face of Northern cities.

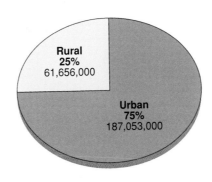

Urban and Rural Populations in 1990

Rural
25%
61,656,000

Urban
75%
187,053,000

1963
Martin Luther King gives his "I Have a Dream" speech.

1969
U.S. astronauts walk on the moon.

Now

The Fourth Wave of Immigration, 1950–Now

The latest wave of immigrants differs from the previous waves. No longer are most of the newcomers from Europe. Most are from Asia and Latin America. As in the Third Wave, the new immigrants are changing the ethnic character of American cities.

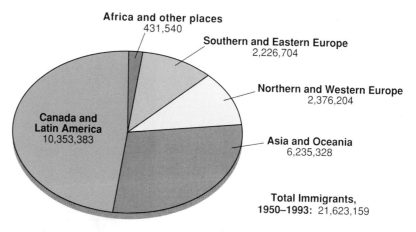

Africa and other places
431,540

Southern and Eastern Europe
2,226,704

Northern and Western Europe
2,376,204

Asia and Oceania
6,235,328

Canada and Latin America
10,353,383

Total Immigrants, 1950–1993: 21,623,159

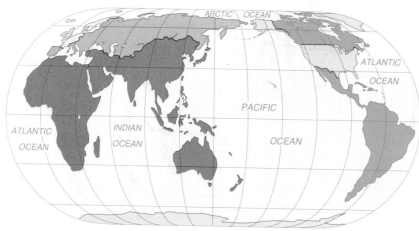

Origins of Immigrants to the United States, 1950–Now

- Northern and Western Europe
- Southern and Eastern Europe*
- Africa
- Asia and Oceania
- Canada and Latin America

*Includes Russian Siberia

Names of major immigrant groups are shown like this: **MEXICAN**

The influence of Spanish-speaking immigrants can be seen in neighborhood street signs. Throughout our history, newcomers have moved into ethnic communities.

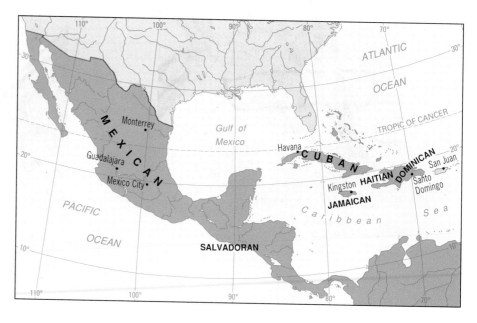

1950–1953
U.S. troops fight in the Korean War.

1961–1963
John F. Kennedy serves as the 35th President.

1950

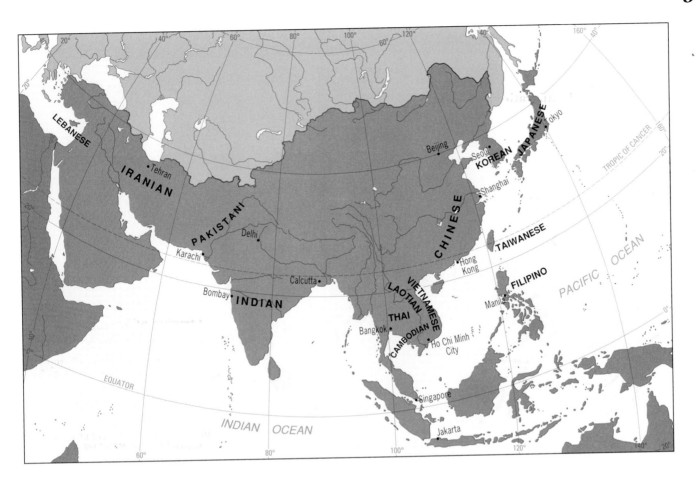

LEBANESE

IRANIAN

•Tehran

PAKISTANI

Karachi•

•Delhi

Bombay•INDIAN

Calcutta•

INDIAN   OCEAN

•Bangkok

THAI

CAMBODIAN

LAOTIAN

VIETNAMESE

•Ho Chi Minh
City

•Singapore

•Jakarta

CHINESE

Beijing•

Shanghai•

•Hong
Kong

Seoul• KOREAN JAPANESE

•Tokyo

TAIWANESE

FILIPINO

Manila•

PACIFIC   OCEAN

TROPIC OF CANCER

EQUATOR

Since 1960, hundreds of thousands of Haitians and
Cubans have sought refuge in the United States.
Many risked crossing the sea in small boats.

Like other immigrants, young Asian students must learn
English in addition to their other subjects.

1961–1973
U.S. troops fight in the Vietnam War.

1981
IBM introduces its PC and personal
computers become widespread.

1989–1991
Communist governments collapse
in Eastern Europe.

Now

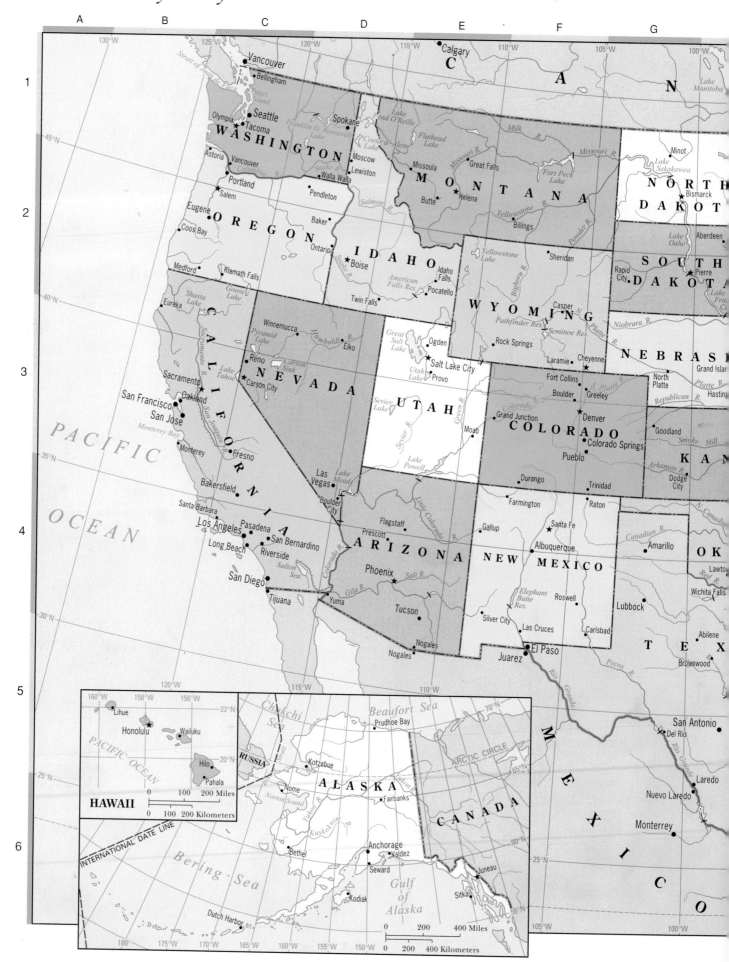

UNITED STATES Political

BOUNDARIES

International boundary

State boundary

CITIES

● Chicago

● Anchorage

• Boulder

A city's relative size is shown by the size of its symbol and lettering.

⊛ Washington, D.C. National capital

★ Honolulu State capital

| 0 | 100 | 200 | 300 Miles |

| 0 | 100 | 200 | 300 Kilometers |

Complete legend on page 5   Bonne projection

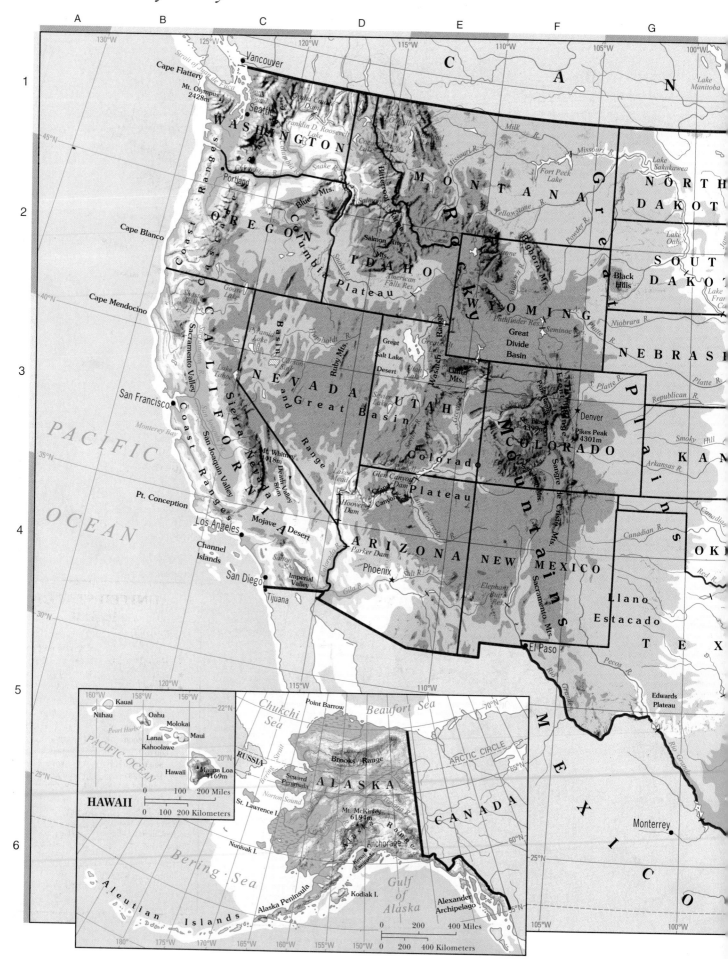

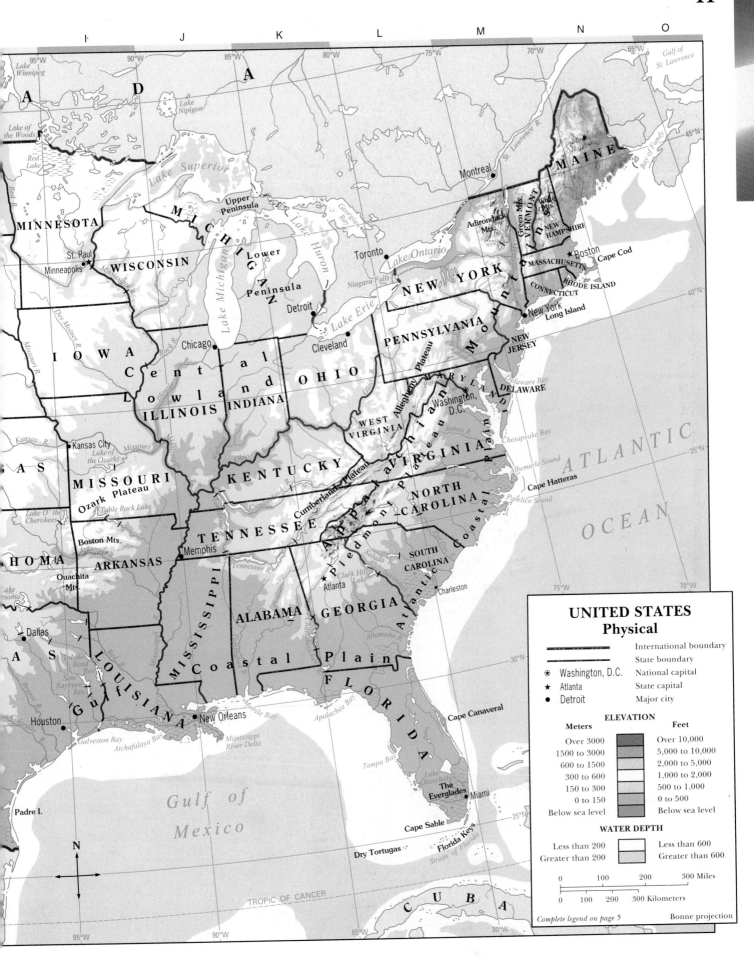

I J K L M N O

CANADA

Lake Winnipeg
Lake of the Woods
Red Lake
Red R.
Lake Nipigon
Lake Superior

MINNESOTA
St. Paul
Minneapolis
Mississippi R.

WISCONSIN

MICHIGAN
Upper Peninsula
Lower Peninsula
Lake Michigan
Lake Huron
Georgian Bay
Lake Ontario
Toronto
Niagara Falls
Lake Erie
Detroit
Cleveland

Montreal
St. Lawrence R.
Gulf of St. Lawrence

MAINE
Moosehead Lake
Lake Champlain
Green Mts.
White Mts.
VERMONT
NEW HAMPSHIRE
Adirondack Mts.
Bay of Fundy

NEW YORK
Boston
MASSACHUSETTS
Cape Cod
CONNECTICUT
RHODE ISLAND
New York
Long Island

IOWA
Des Moines R.
Missouri R.

Central Lowland

ILLINOIS **INDIANA**
Chicago
Rock R.
Illinois R.

OHIO

PENNSYLVANIA
Allegheny Plateau

NEW JERSEY
Delaware Bay
DELAWARE
MARYLAND
Washington, D.C.
WEST VIRGINIA
James R.
Chesapeake Bay

Kansas R.
Kansas City
Lake of the Ozarks
Missouri R.

MISSOURI
Ozark Plateau
Table Rock Lake

KENTUCKY
Ohio R.
Cumberland Plateau
Cumberland R.

VIRGINIA
Roanoke R.
Piedmont
Albemarle Sound
Cape Hatteras
Pamlico Sound

ATLANTIC OCEAN

Lake O' the Cherokees

OKLAHOMA
Boston Mts.
Ouachita Mts.
Arkansas R.

ARKANSAS
Memphis
Tennessee R.

TENNESSEE
Appalachian Mountains

NORTH CAROLINA
Atlantic Coastal Plain
Saluda R.
SOUTH CAROLINA
Clark Hill Lake
★ Atlanta
Charleston

Lake Texoma

TEXAS
Dallas
Red R.
Toledo Bend Res.
Sam Rayburn Res.
Brazos R.
Colorado R.
Houston
Galveston Bay
Padre I.
Atchafalaya Bay

LOUISIANA
MISSISSIPPI
ALABAMA
GEORGIA
Chattahoochee R.
Altamaha R.
New Orleans
Mobile Bay
Apalachee Bay
Mississippi River Delta

Coastal Plain

Gulf of Mexico

FLORIDA
Tampa Bay
Lake Okeechobee
The Everglades
Miami
Cape Canaveral
Cape Sable
Florida Keys
Straits of Florida
Dry Tortugas

TROPIC OF CANCER

CUBA

N

UNITED STATES
Physical

————	International boundary
————	State boundary
⊛ Washington, D.C.	National capital
★ Atlanta	State capital
● Detroit	Major city

ELEVATION

Meters		Feet
Over 3000		Over 10,000
1500 to 3000		5,000 to 10,000
600 to 1500		2,000 to 5,000
300 to 600		1,000 to 2,000
150 to 300		500 to 1,000
0 to 150		0 to 500
Below sea level		Below sea level

WATER DEPTH

Less than 200		Less than 600
Greater than 200		Greater than 600

0   100   200   300 Miles
0   100   200   300 Kilometers

Complete legend on page 5   Bonne projection

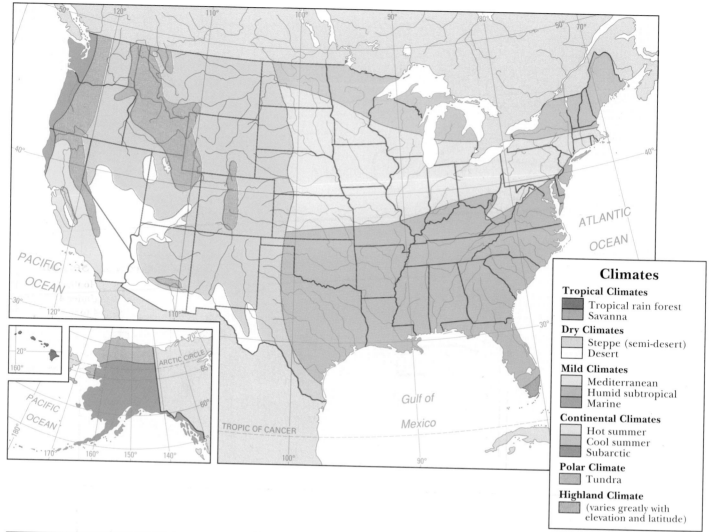

Climates

Tropical Climates
- Tropical rain forest
- Savanna

Dry Climates
- Steppe (semi-desert)
- Desert

Mild Climates
- Mediterranean
- Humid subtropical
- Marine

Continental Climates
- Hot summer
- Cool summer
- Subarctic

Polar Climate
- Tundra

Highland Climate
- (varies greatly with elevation and latitude)

Steppe climates get enough rain for short grass, but not enough for trees.

Humid subtropical climates have hot, wet summers and mild, damp winters.

Marine climates are warm in summer, and cool and rainy the rest of the year.

Hot summer climates have hot, rainy summers and cold, snowy winters.

Cool summer climates have cool, rainy summers and cold, very snowy winters.

Climates

The climate of a place is its typical weather in all seasons.

Two conditions are most useful for describing climate. One is average temperatures in different seasons. The other is average annual rainfall, which also includes snow. Ten inches of snow is counted as one inch of rain.

The United States is so large that it has several distinct climates. How many can you count in just the 48 contiguous states?

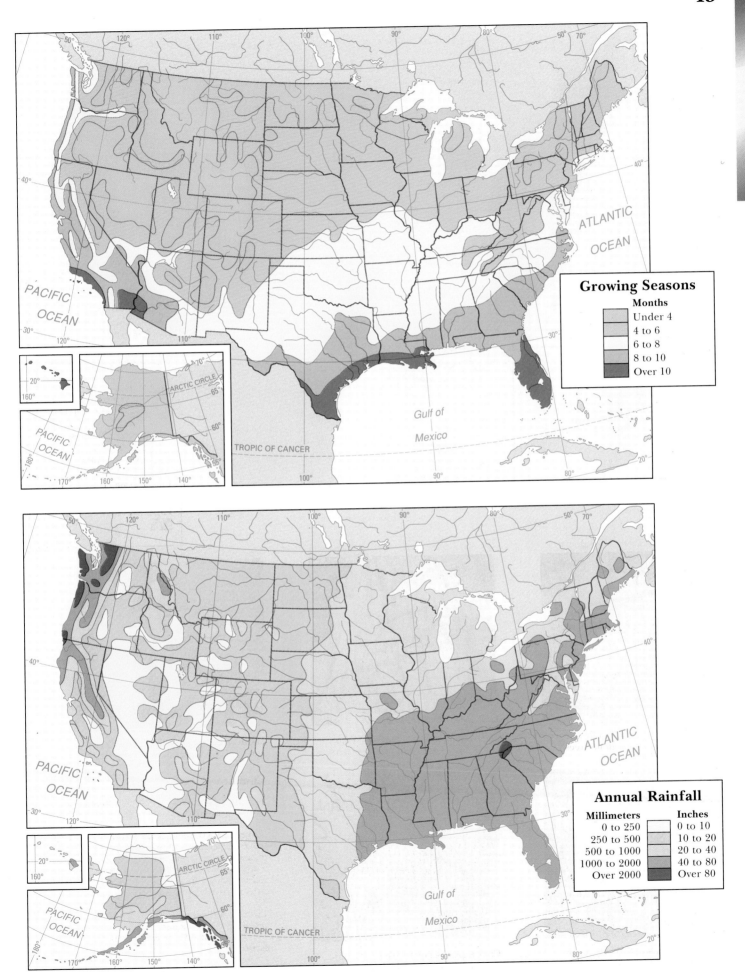

Growing Seasons

Months
- Under 4
- 4 to 6
- 6 to 8
- 8 to 10
- Over 10

Annual Rainfall

Millimeters	Inches
0 to 250	0 to 10
250 to 500	10 to 20
500 to 1000	20 to 40
1000 to 2000	40 to 80
Over 2000	Over 80

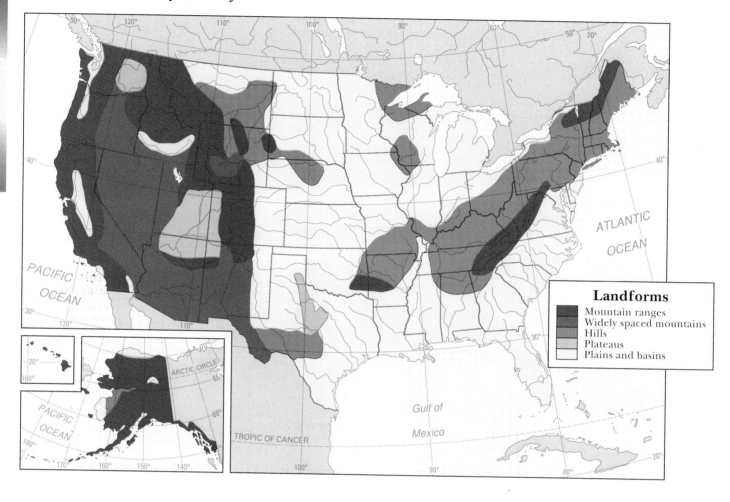

Landforms

- Mountain ranges
- Widely spaced mountains
- Hills
- Plateaus
- Plains and basins

ATLANTIC OCEAN

PACIFIC OCEAN

Gulf of Mexico

TROPIC OF CANCER

ARCTIC CIRCLE

PACIFIC OCEAN

Mountain ranges may be hundreds, even thousands of miles long.

Widely spaced mountains rise above valley floors in many western states.

Hills usually are not too tall, but some "hills" really are low mountains.

Plateaus, like the Colorado Plateau, are often deeply cut by canyons.

Plains may be flat land or they may be land that is gently rolling.

Landforms

All the landforms of the United States are variations of those shown here.

Some mountains are steep, rugged, and very high. But older mountains are worn down, smoother, and lower.

Hills of one height or another are found in every region of the country.

Plateaus are high, mostly level lands that often are deeply cut by rivers.

Plains can be found in any climate region. A basin is a kind of plain surrounded by higher land.

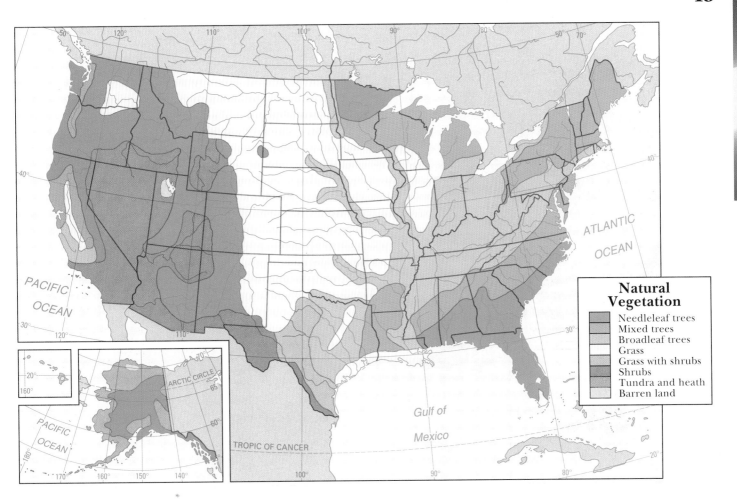

Natural Vegetation

Needleleaf trees
Mixed trees
Broadleaf trees
Grass
Grass with shrubs
Shrubs
Tundra and heath
Barren land

Needleleaf trees often are called evergreens because most remain green all year.

Mixed trees include evergreens and broadleaf trees, which change color in fall.

Grass, the dominant plant of the prairies, is often dotted with wildflowers.

Shrubs like cactus and yucca are common in dry parts of the country.

Tundra and heath plants are short and thrive in the brief summers of Alaska.

Natural Vegetation

The United States can be divided into large regions sharing the same natural vegetation. That is the plant life that would dominate a region if it were not for the changes people bring.

Many areas were once forests but are now planted with crops and paved over with cities. Similarly, natural prairie grasses are disappearing.

Yet natural vegetation categories tell much about climates and still describe the look of many places.

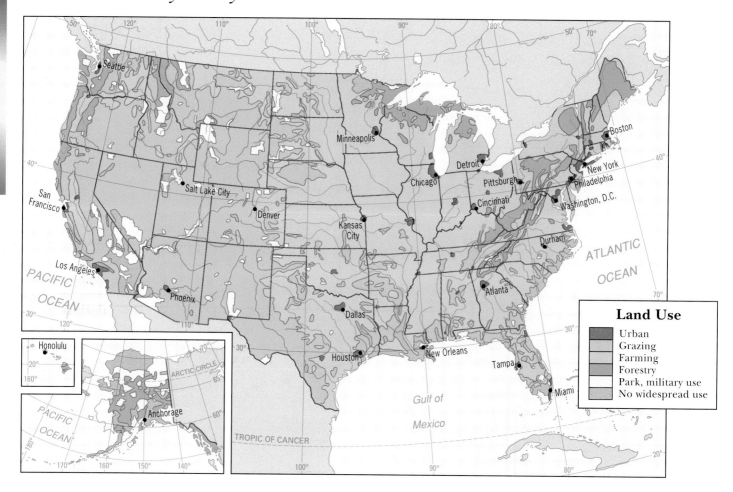

Land Use
- Urban
- Grazing
- Farming
- Forestry
- Park, military use
- No widespread use

Urban areas now include more people living in suburbs than in central cities.

Grazing animals raised in the United States are mainly cattle and sheep.

Farming means growing crops or raising livestock for sale to others.

Forestry provides lumber for houses and wood pulp for paper.

No widespread use most often describes very dry, very wet, or very cold places.

Land Use

The United States can be divided according to patterns of land use.

On the map, a region's name describes its most common use, although there may be other uses that are less widespread.

A land use name may describe many different but related activities. Farming, for example, can refer to many kinds of crops or livestock or both.

Some land uses require certain climates. But cities are found even where it is too wet or too dry for other uses.

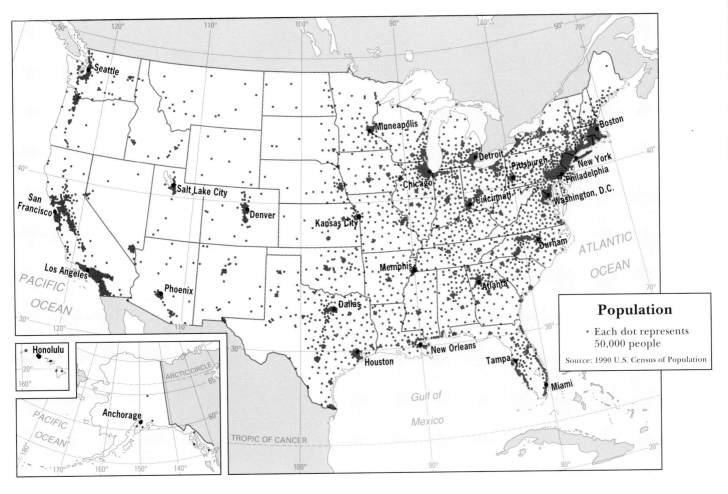

Population

- Each dot represents
  50,000 people

Source: 1990 U.S. Census of Population

Ethnic Population in 1990

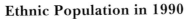

Few
Some
Many

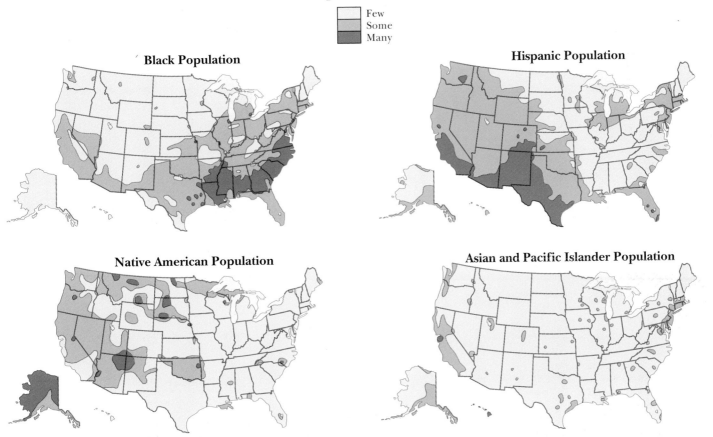

Black Population

Hispanic Population

Native American Population

Asian and Pacific Islander Population

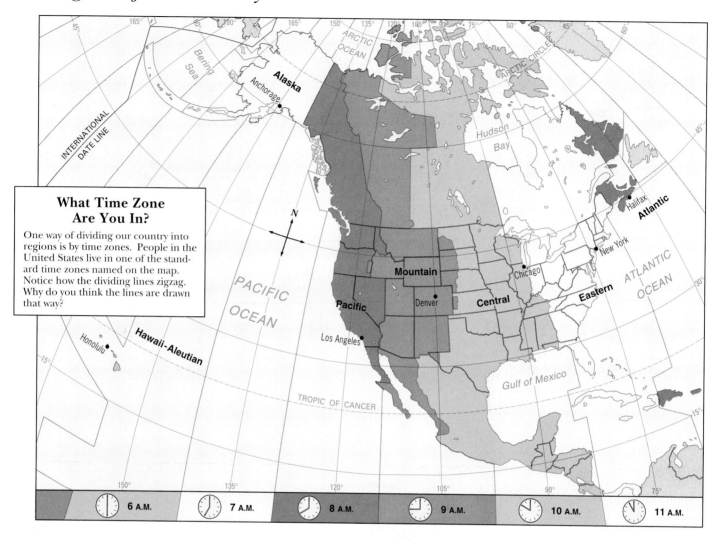

What Time Zone Are You In?

One way of dividing our country into regions is by time zones. People in the United States live in one of the standard time zones named on the map. Notice how the dividing lines zigzag. Why do you think the lines are drawn that way?

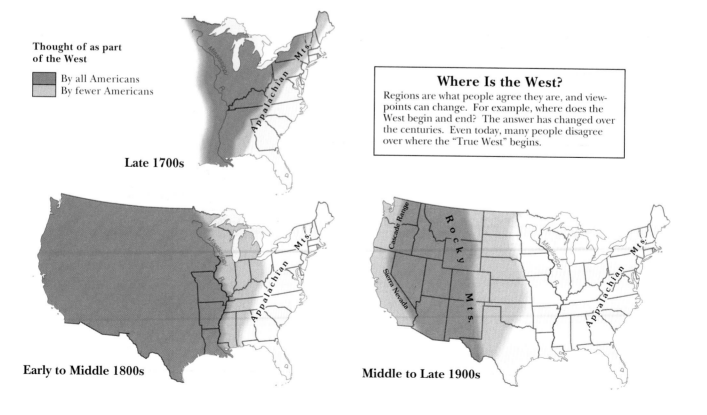

Thought of as part of the West

By all Americans
By fewer Americans

Late 1700s

Where Is the West?

Regions are what people agree they are, and viewpoints can change. For example, where does the West begin and end? The answer has changed over the centuries. Even today, many people disagree over where the "True West" begins.

Early to Middle 1800s

Middle to Late 1900s

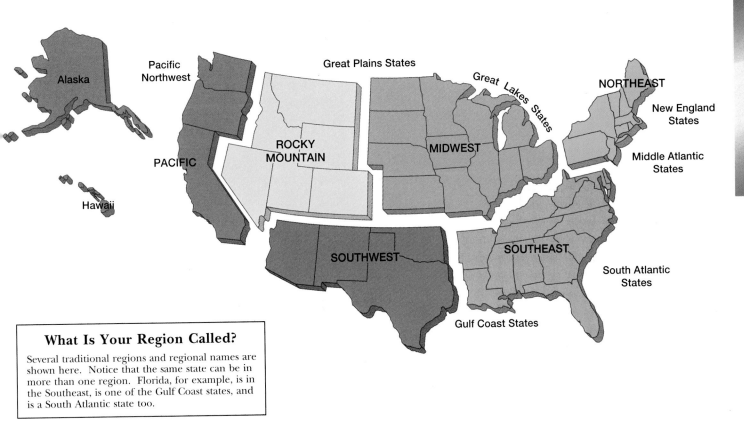

What Is Your Region Called?

Several traditional regions and regional names are shown here. Notice that the same state can be in more than one region. Florida, for example, is in the Southeast, is one of the Gulf Coast states, and is a South Atlantic state too.

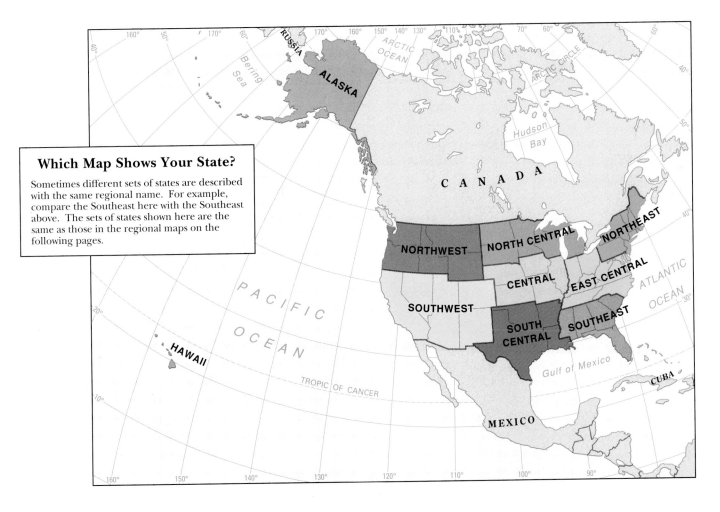

Which Map Shows Your State?

Sometimes different sets of states are described with the same regional name. For example, compare the Southeast here with the Southeast above. The sets of states shown here are the same as those in the regional maps on the following pages.

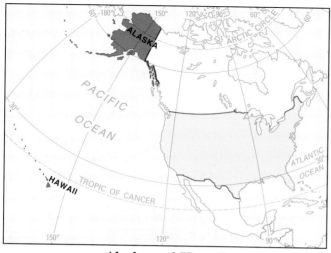

Alaska and Hawaii

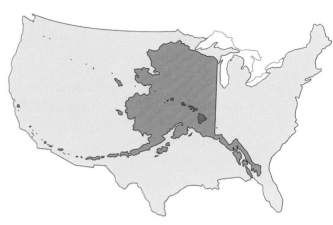

Alaska and Hawaii Area Comparison

Hawaii	6,459 sq. mi.	(16 729 sq. km)
Alaska	591,004 sq. mi.	(1 530 693 sq. km)
Contiguous U.S.	3,021,295 sq. mi.	(7 825 112 sq. km)

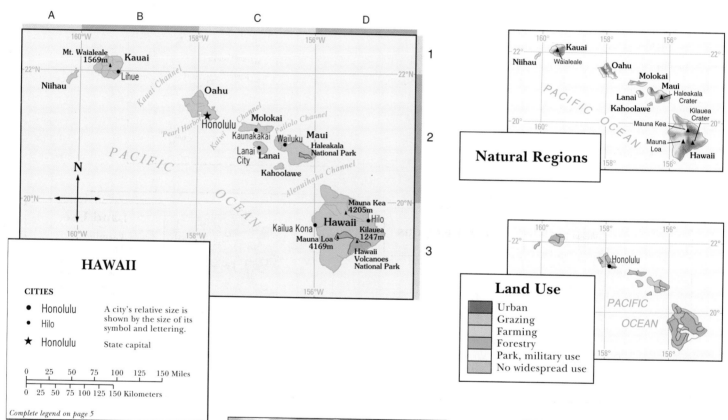

HAWAII

CITIES

● Honolulu — A city's relative size is shown by the size of its symbol and lettering.

● Hilo

★ Honolulu — State capital

| 0 | 25 | 50 | 75 | 100 | 125 | 150 Miles |

| 0 | 25 | 50 | 75 | 100 | 125 | 150 Kilometers |

Complete legend on page 5

Natural Regions

Land Use

- Urban
- Grazing
- Farming
- Forestry
- Park, military use
- No widespread use

The sun bounces off Honolulu's Waikiki Beach. Diamond Head, an extinct volcano, is the dark mass in the background.

Waterfalls interrupt the lush greenery of Hawaii's tropical rain forests.

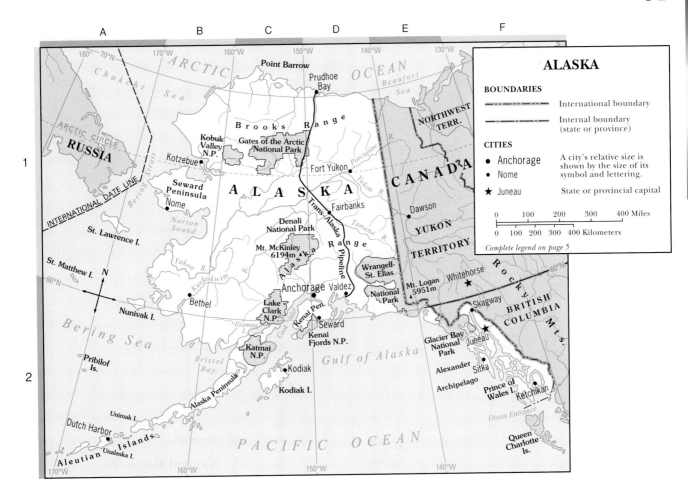

ALASKA

BOUNDARIES

International boundary

Internal boundary
(state or province)

CITIES

● Anchorage — A city's relative size is shown by the size of its symbol and lettering.
● Nome

★ Juneau — State or provincial capital

0   100   200   300   400 Miles

0   100   200   300   400 Kilometers

Complete legend on page 5

Natural Regions

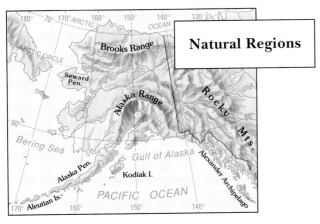

Land Use

Farming
Forestry
Park, military use
No widespread use

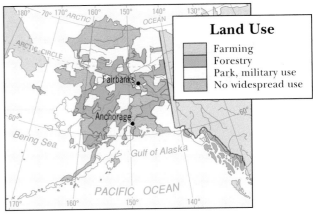

In Kenai Fiords National Park, massive glaciers reach Alaska's coast.

Mt. McKinley towers over one of Alaska's many wilderness areas.

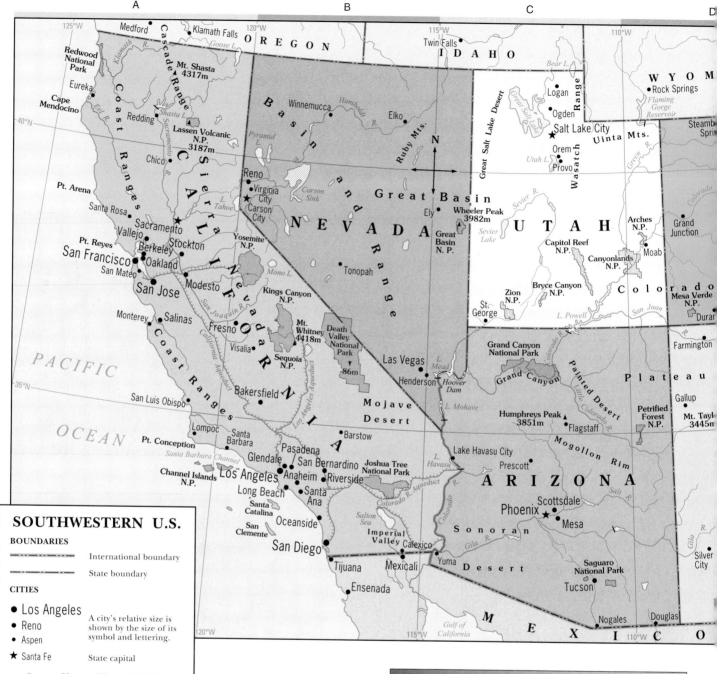

A   **B**   **C**   **D**

OREGON   IDAHO

WYOM

Medford ·   · Klamath Falls   · Twin Falls

Redwood National Park

Eureka ·

Cape Mendocino ·

Mt. Shasta 4317m

Cascade Range

Coast Ranges

Klamath R.

Shasta L.

Redding ·

· Chico

Lassen Volcanic N.P. 3187m

Sierra Nevada Range

C A L I F O R N I A

Pt. Arena ·

Santa Rosa ·

Sacramento ★

Vallejo ·

Pt. Reyes ·

Berkeley · Stockton ·

San Francisco ·

Oakland ·

San Mateo ·

San Jose ·

Modesto ·

Monterey ·

Salinas ·

Fresno ·

Visalia ·

Bakersfield ·

San Luis Obispo ·

Yosemite N.P.

Mono L.

Kings Canyon N.P.

Mt. Whitney 4418m

Sequoia N.P.

San Joaquin R.

California Aqueduct

Los Angeles Aqueduct

PACIFIC

OCEAN

Lompoc ·

Pt. Conception ·

Santa Barbara ·

Channel Islands N.P.

Glendale ·

Los Angeles ·

Pasadena ·

San Bernardino ·

Anaheim ·

Riverside ·

Santa Ana ·

Long Beach ·

Santa Catalina

San Clemente

Oceanside ·

San Diego ·

Tijuana ·

Ensenada ·

Winnemucca ·

Humboldt R.

Elko ·

Ruby Mts.

Basin and Range

N E V A D A

Reno ·

Virginia City ★

Carson City ★

L. Tahoe

Pyramid L.

Carson Sink

Tonopah ·

Great Basin

Ely ·   Wheeler Peak 3982m

Great Basin N.P.

Death Valley National Park -86m

Las Vegas ·

Henderson ·

Hoover Dam

L. Mead

L. Mohave

Mojave Desert

Barstow ·

Joshua Tree National Park

Salton Sea

Imperial Valley

Calexico

Mexicali ·

Yuma ·

Gulf of California

N

U T A H

Great Salt Lake Desert

Logan ·

Ogden ·

Great Salt Lake

Salt Lake City ★

Orem · Provo ·

Utah L.

Wasatch Range

Uinta Mts.

Sevier R.

Sevier Lake

Capitol Reef N.P.

Zion N.P.

St. George ·

Bryce Canyon N.P.

Canyonlands N.P.

L. Powell

Arches N.P.

Moab ·

San Juan R.

Grand Canyon National Park

Grand Canyon

Colorado R.

Painted Desert

Little Colorado R.

Plateau

Humphreys Peak 3851m

Flagstaff ·

Prescott ·

Lake Havasu City ·

L. Havasu

Colorado R. Aqueduct

A R I Z O N A

Mogollon Rim

Petrified Forest N.P.

Gallup ·

Mt. Tayl 3445m

Phoenix ★

Scottsdale ·

Mesa ·

Sonoran

Saguaro National Park

Gila R.

Desert

Tucson ·

Nogales ·

Douglas ·

Rock Springs ·

Flaming Gorge Reservoir

Steamb Spri

Uinta Mts.

Green R.

Colorado

C o l o r a d o

Grand Junction ·

Mesa Verde N.P.

Durar

Farmington ·

Silver City ·

Salt R.

Gila R.

M E X I C O

125°W   120°W   115°W   110°W

40°N   35°N

SOUTHWESTERN U.S.

BOUNDARIES

—··—··—   International boundary

————   State boundary

CITIES

● **Los Angeles**

● Reno

· Aspen

A city's relative size is shown by the size of its symbol and lettering.

★ Santa Fe   State capital

0   50   100   150 Miles

0   50   100   150 Kilometers

Complete legend on page 5

Spectacular rock formations caused by weathering are seen in Utah at Arches National Park.

On a clear night, San Francisco glitters at the end of the Golden Gate Bridge.

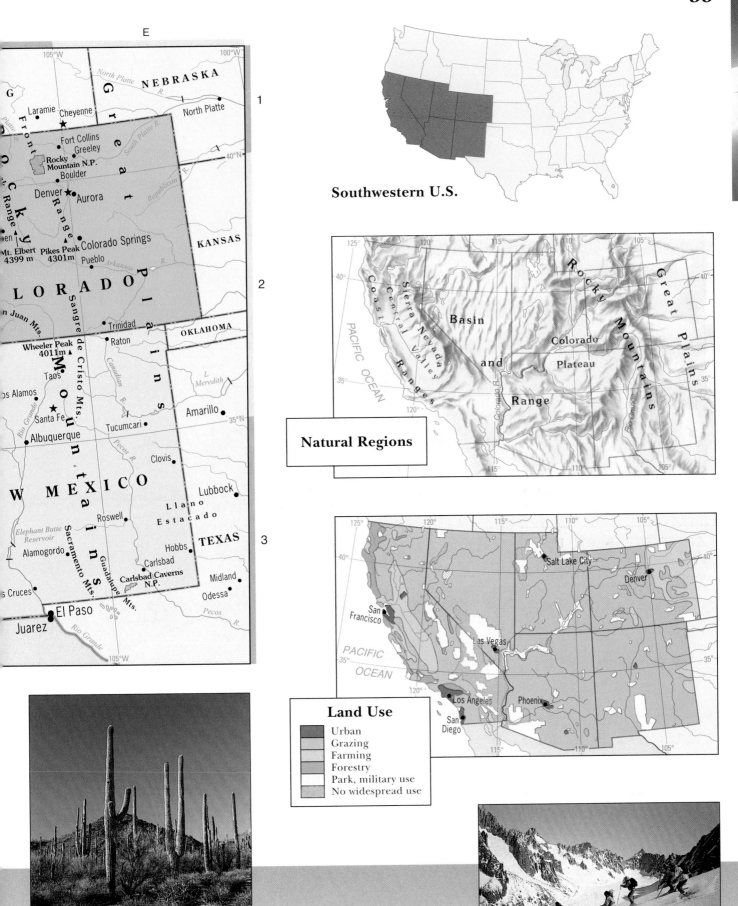

E

NEBRASKA

Laramie Cheyenne ★ North Platte

North Platte R.

1

Fort Collins
Greeley

Rocky
Mountain N.P.
Boulder

40°N

Denver ★ Aurora

South Platte R.

Republican R.

KANSAS

2

Mt. Elbert Pikes Peak Colorado Springs
4399 m 4301m

Pueblo

Arkansas R.

LORADO

Sangre de Cristo Mts.

Trinidad

OKLAHOMA

n Juan Mts.

Wheeler Peak
4011m ▲ Raton

Canadian R.

L.
Meredith

os Alamos Taos

Amarillo

35°N

Santa Fe ★

Tucumcari

Pecos R.

Albuquerque

Rio Grande

W MEXICO

Clovis

Lubbock

Roswell

Llano
Estacado

3

Elephant Butte
Reservoir

Alamogordo

Sacramento Mts.

Hobbs

Carlsbad

TEXAS

Midland

s Cruces

Guadalupe Mts.

Carlsbad Caverns
N.P.

Odessa

El Paso

Pecos R.

Juarez

Rio Grande

105°W

105°W 100°W

Southwestern U.S.

Natural Regions

Coast Ranges
Sierra Nevada
Central Valley
PACIFIC OCEAN
Basin
and
Range
Colorado R.
Colorado
Plateau
Rocky Mountains
Great Plains
Rio Grande

Land Use

Salt Lake City

Denver

San
Francisco

Las Vegas

PACIFIC

OCEAN

Los Angeles

Phoenix

San
Diego

▨	Urban
▨	Grazing
▨	Farming
▨	Forestry
☐	Park, military use
▨	No widespread use

Giant saguaro cacti flourish in
Arizona's desert country.

Deep snow and steep slopes
attract skiers from all over the
world to the Colorado Rockies.

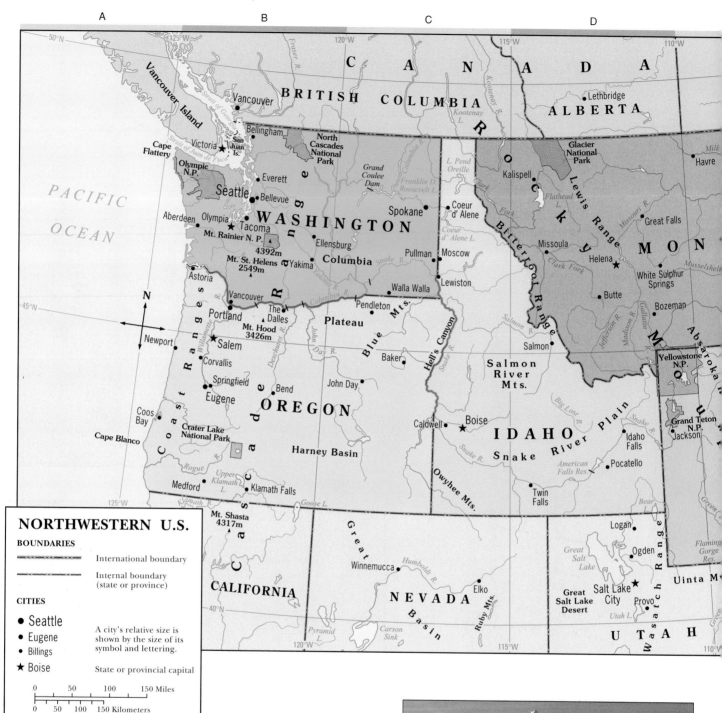

NORTHWESTERN U.S.

BOUNDARIES

————— International boundary

————— Internal boundary
(state or province)

CITIES

● Seattle

● Eugene

● Billings

★ Boise

A city's relative size is shown by the size of its symbol and lettering.

State or provincial capital

0   50   100   150 Miles

0   50   100   150 Kilometers

Complete legend on page 5

Seattle's Space Needle rises above the city. Mt. Rainier shines in the distance.

Quiet in the Wyoming winter, Grand Teton National Park is blanketed with snow.

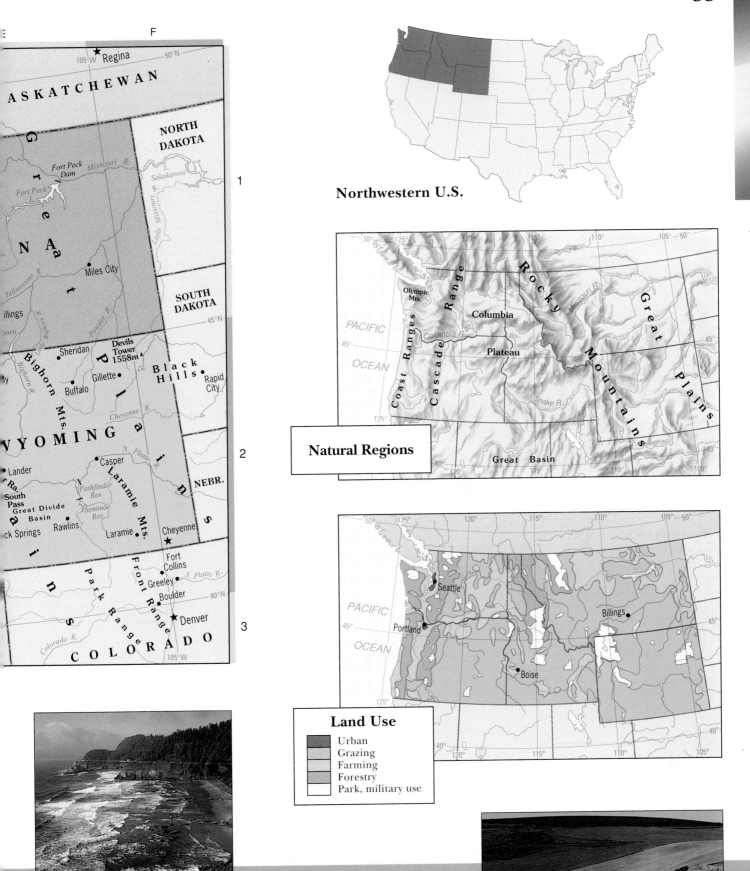

Northwestern U.S.

Natural Regions

PACIFIC OCEAN

Coast Ranges

Cascade Range

Olympic Mts.

Rocky Mountains

Columbia

Plateau

Great Plains

Columbia R.

Missouri R.

Snake R.

Great Basin

Land Use

- Urban
- Grazing
- Farming
- Forestry
- Park, military use

PACIFIC OCEAN

Seattle

Portland

Boise

Billings

E **F**

Regina

105°W 50°N

S A S K A T C H E W A N

G r e a t

N A

a

t

NORTH DAKOTA

Fort Peck Dam

Fort Peck L.

Missouri R.

L. Sakakawea

Little Missouri R.

Miles City

Yellowstone R.

Billings

Powder R.

SOUTH DAKOTA

45°N

Sheridan

Bighorn R.

Bighorn Mts.

Devils Tower 1558m

Buffalo Gillette

B l a c k H i l l s

Rapid City

P l a i n s

Cheyenne R.

W Y O M I N G

Casper

N. Platte R.

Laramie Mts.

NEBR.

Lander

South Pass

Great Divide Basin

Pathfinder Res.

Seminoe Res.

ck Springs Rawlins

Laramie

Cheyenne

Fort Collins

S. Platte R.

Greeley

Park Range

Front Range

Boulder

40°N

Denver

Colorado R.

C O L O R A D O

105°W

1

2

3

Oregon's coast is known for pounding waves and sudden mists.

Wheat fields sprawl across the rolling plains of the Columbia Plateau.

North Central U.S.

Natural Regions

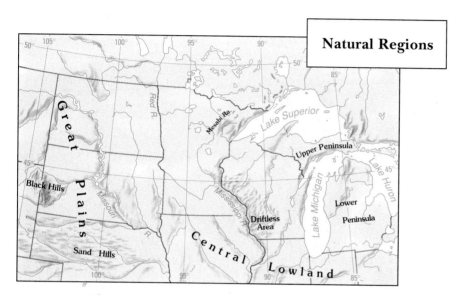

Land Use

■	Urban
■	Grazing
■	Farming
■	Forestry
□	Park, military use
■	No widespread use

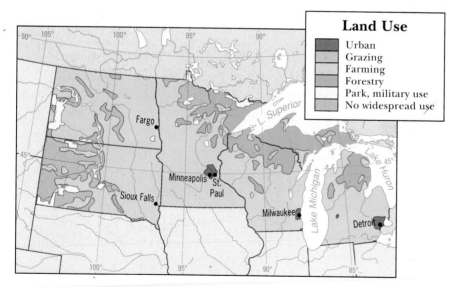

Holsteins are the favored breed of cow on the dairy farms of Wisconsin, Minnesota, and Michigan.

Four Presidents are carved from the rock of Mount Rushmore. Can you name them?

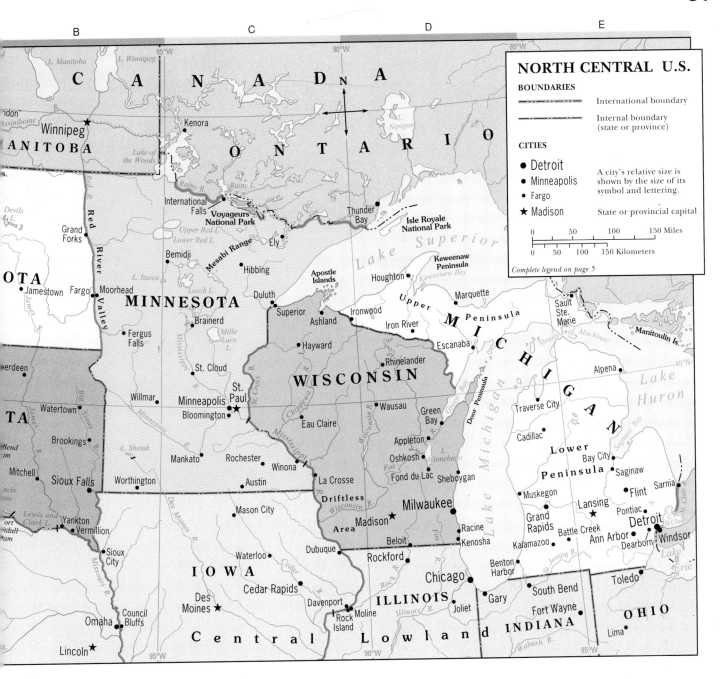

NORTH CENTRAL U.S.

BOUNDARIES

International boundary

Internal boundary
(state or province)

CITIES

● **Detroit**

● **Minneapolis**

• Fargo

★ Madison

A city's relative size is
shown by the size of its
symbol and lettering.

State or provincial capital

0 50 100 150 Miles

0 50 100 150 Kilometers

Complete legend on page 5

C A N A D A

ndon

l. Manitoba L. Winnipeg

M A N I T O B A

Winnipeg

O N T A R I O

Kenora

Lake of
the Woods

L. Nipigon

Devils
L.

Grand
Forks

Red River Valley

O T A

Jamestown

Fargo Moorhead

James R.

MINNESOTA

Fergus
Falls

L. Itasca

Leech L.

Mille
Lacs
L.

St. Cloud

Brainerd

Bemidji

Rainy R. Rainy L.

International
Falls **Voyageurs
National Park**

Upper Red L.
Lower Red L.

Mesabi Range

Hibbing

Ely

Duluth

Superior

Thunder
Bay

**Isle Royale
National Park**

Lake Superior

Apostle
Islands

Ashland

Ironwood

Iron River

Keweenaw
Peninsula

Keweenaw Bay

Houghton

Marquette

Escanaba

Upper Peninsula

M I C H I G A N

Sault
Ste.
Marie

Manitoulin Is.

Straits of Mackinac

Aberdeen

Big Sioux R.

Watertown

Brookings

L. Shetak

T A

Minnesota R.

Willmar

Minneapolis St. Paul

Bloomington

Mankato

Rochester

Hayward

Rhinelander

WISCONSIN

St. Croix R.

Chippewa R.

Eau Claire

Wausau

Wisconsin R.

Green
Bay

Door Peninsula

Green Bay

Appleton

Oshkosh

Fox R.

L.
Winnebago

Fond du Lac

Sheboygan

Alpena

Traverse City

Cadillac

**Lower
Peninsula**

Lake Huron

Lake Michigan

Saginaw Bay

Bay City

Saginaw

Sarnia

Muskegon

Flint

Grand
Rapids

Lansing

Pontiac

Battle Creek

Kalamazoo

Detroit

Windsor

Ann Arbor Dearborn

L.
St. Clair

Bend
m

Mitchell

James R.

Francis
ase
R.

Sioux Falls

Worthington

Mason City

Winona

La Crosse

Driftless

Wisconsin R.

Area Madison

Beloit

Milwaukee

Racine

Kenosha

Rock R.

Fort
dall
am

Lewis and
Clark L.

Yankton

Vermillion

Missouri R.

Des Moines R.

Cedar R.

Waterloo

I O W A

Mason City

Austin

Dubuque

Rockford

Benton
Harbor

Lake
Erie

Toledo

O H I O

Sioux
City

Cedar Rapids

Des
Moines

Davenport

Rock
Island Moline

Illinois R.

ILLINOIS

Chicago

Gary

South Bend

Fort Wayne

INDIANA

Lima

St. Joseph R.

Omaha

Council
Bluffs

Lincoln

Central Lowland

Joliet

Wabash R.

95°W 90°W 85°W

45°N

A quiet old neighborhood in Milwaukee has
architecture that shows a European influence.

Michigan has 3,288 miles of shoreline along the Great Lakes,
which hold the largest supply of fresh water in the world.

Central U.S.

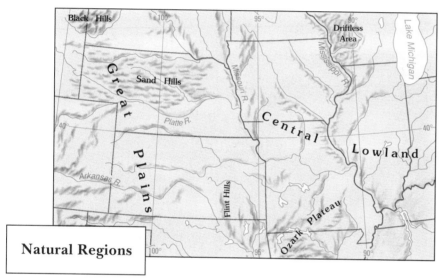

Natural Regions

Black Hills
Driftless Area
Sand Hills
Great Plains
Central Lowland
Missouri R.
Mississippi R.
Lake Michigan
Platte R.
Arkansas R.
Flint Hills
Ozark Plateau

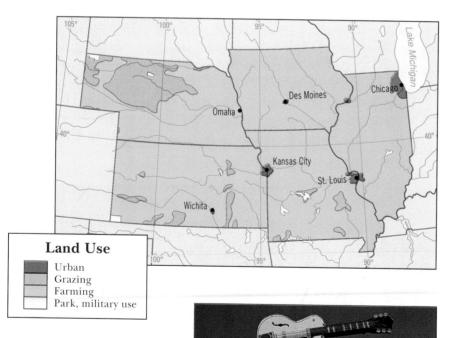

Land Use
- Urban
- Grazing
- Farming
- Park, military use

Des Moines
Chicago
Omaha
Kansas City
St. Louis
Wichita
Lake Michigan

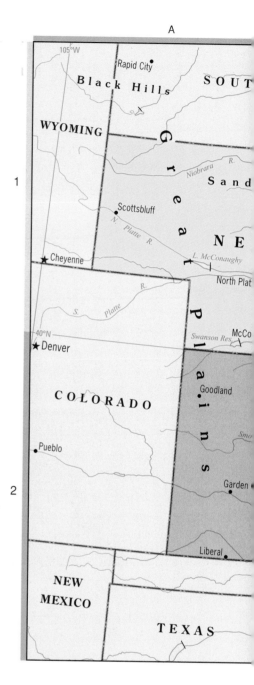

A
105°W
Rapid City
Black Hills
SOUT
WYOMING
G r e a t
Sand
N E
Niobrara R.
Scottsbluff
N. Platte R.
Cheyenne
L. McConaughy
North Plat
S. Platte R.
40°N
Denver
Swanson Res.
McCo
COLORADO
P l a i n s
Goodland
Pueblo
Garden
Smo
Liberal
NEW MEXICO
TEXAS

Country-music theaters attract 5 million visitors to Branson, Missouri, each year.

Storm clouds gather over a field of millet on the Great Plains.

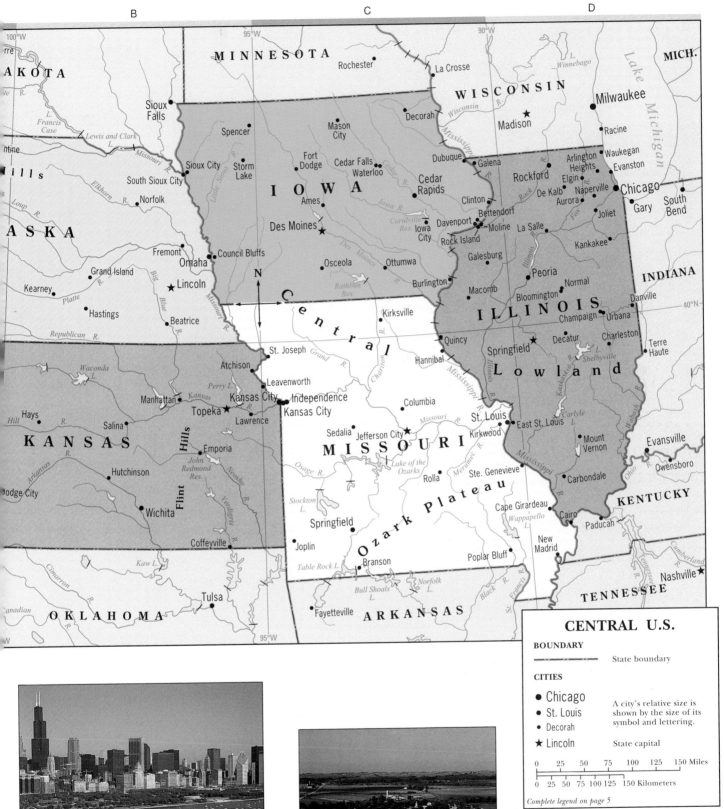

B   C   D

100°W

MINNESOTA

95°W

90°W

MICH.

AKOTA

Rochester

La Crosse

L. Winnebago

Lake Michigan

L. Francis Case

Lewis and Clark L.

Sioux Falls

Spencer

Mason City

Decorah

WISCONSIN

Wisconsin R.

Madison

Milwaukee

Racine

ills

tine

White R.

Missouri R.

Elkhorn R.

Little Sioux R.

Fort Dodge

Cedar Falls
Waterloo

Cedar R.

Dubuque

Galena

Rockford

Arlington Heights

Waukegan
Evanston

ASKA

Sioux City

Storm Lake

IOWA

Cedar Rapids

Clinton

De Kalb

Elgin

Naperville

Chicago

South Sioux City

Norfolk

Ames

Iowa R.

Bettendorf

Aurora

Gary

South Bend

Loup R.

Fremont

Des Moines

Coralville Res.

Iowa City

Davenport
Moline

La Salle

Joliet

Grand Island

Omaha

Council Bluffs

Rock Island

Fox R.

Kankakee

INDIANA

Kearney

Lincoln

N

Osceola

Des Moines R.

Ottumwa

Galesburg

Peoria

Normal

Danville

40°N

Platte R.

Big Blue R.

Hastings

Beatrice

Rathbun Res.

Burlington

Macomb

Bloomington

ILLINOIS

Champaign

Urbana

Republican R.

Missouri R.

Central

Kirksville

Quincy

Illinois R.

Springfield

Decatur

Charleston

Terre Haute

Waconda L.

St. Joseph

Grand R.

Hannibal

Mississippi R.

Lowland

L. Shelbyville

Atchison

Perry L.

Leavenworth

Chariton R.

Kaskaskia R.

Wabash R.

Manhattan

Kansas R.

Kansas City

Independence

Columbia

Missouri R.

St. Louis

Carlyle L.

Topeka

Lawrence

Sedalia

Jefferson City

Kirkwood

East St. Louis

Mount Vernon

Evansville

Hays

Hill R.

Salina

MISSOURI

Meramec R.

Ste. Genevieve

Mississippi R.

Owensboro

Emporia

John Redmond Res.

Flint Hills

Osage R.

Lake of the Ozarks

Rolla

Carbondale

Ohio R.

KANSAS

Hutchinson

Neosho R.

Verdigris R.

Stockton L.

Cape Girardeau

KENTUCKY

odge City

Arkansas R.

Wichita

Springfield

Ozark Plateau

Wappapello L.

Cairo

Paducah

Cimarron R.

Coffeyville

Kaw L.

Table Rock L.

Joplin

Branson

Bull Shoals L.

Norfork L.

Poplar Bluff

New Madrid

Black R.

St. Francis R.

Cumberland R.

Nashville

Tennessee R.

Canadian R.

Tulsa

OKLAHOMA

Fayetteville

ARKANSAS

TENNESSEE

95°W

Famous for its lakefront skyline, Chicago is most dramatic when seen from Lake Michigan.

Eldorado, Iowa, is one of the many small farming towns that dot the Central Lowland.

CENTRAL U.S.

BOUNDARY

————————   State boundary

CITIES

● **Chicago**

● St. Louis

· Decorah

★ Lincoln

A city's relative size is shown by the size of its symbol and lettering.

State capital

0   25   50   75   100   125   150 Miles

0   25   50   75   100 125   150 Kilometers

Complete legend on page 5

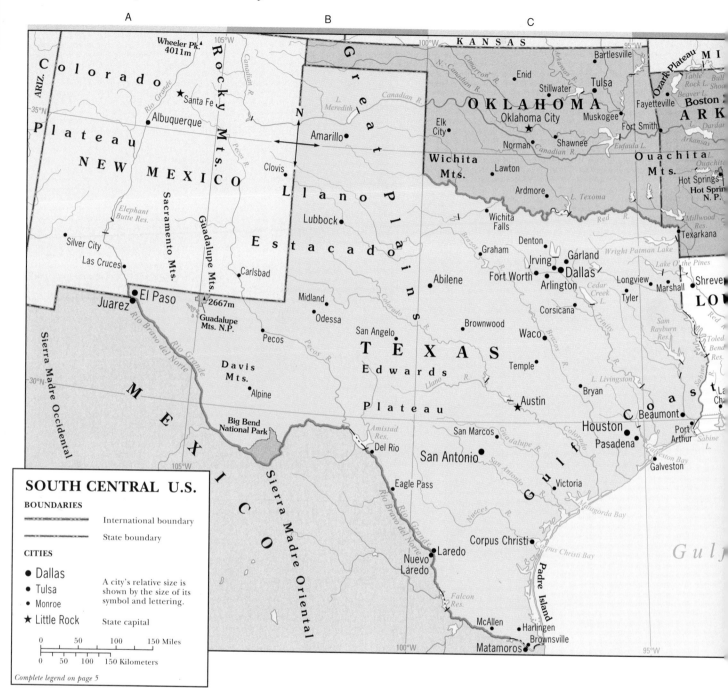

A   B   C

SOUTH CENTRAL U.S.

BOUNDARIES

International boundary

State boundary

CITIES

● **Dallas**

● Tulsa

• Monroe   A city's relative size is
                shown by the size of its
                symbol and lettering.

★ Little Rock   State capital

0   50   100   150 Miles

0   50   100   150 Kilometers

Complete legend on page 5

Desert wildflowers bloom in Big Bend National Park.
The park is along the Rio Grande in western Texas.

Houses hug the low ground along a channel of the Mississippi
Delta in Louisiana. Can you spot the highway?

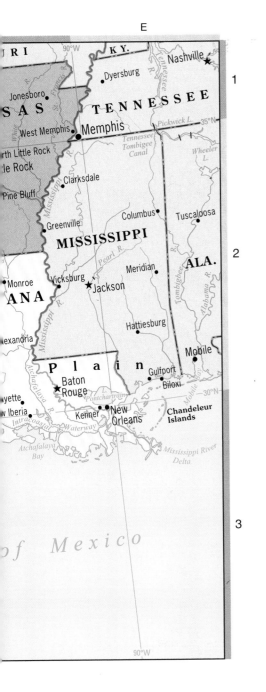

South Central U.S.

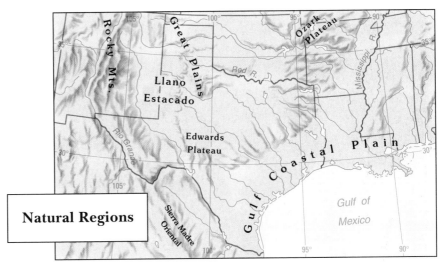

Natural Regions

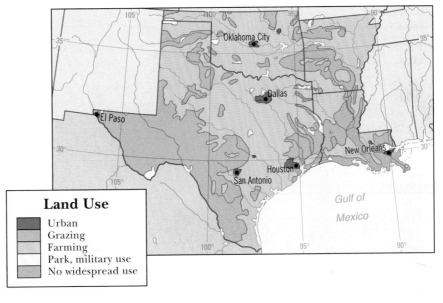

Land Use

- Urban
- Grazing
- Farming
- Park, military use
- No widespread use

A derrick supports heavy drilling equipment for a new oil well in Oklahoma.

It's Mardi Gras! New Orleans celebrates the festival every year.

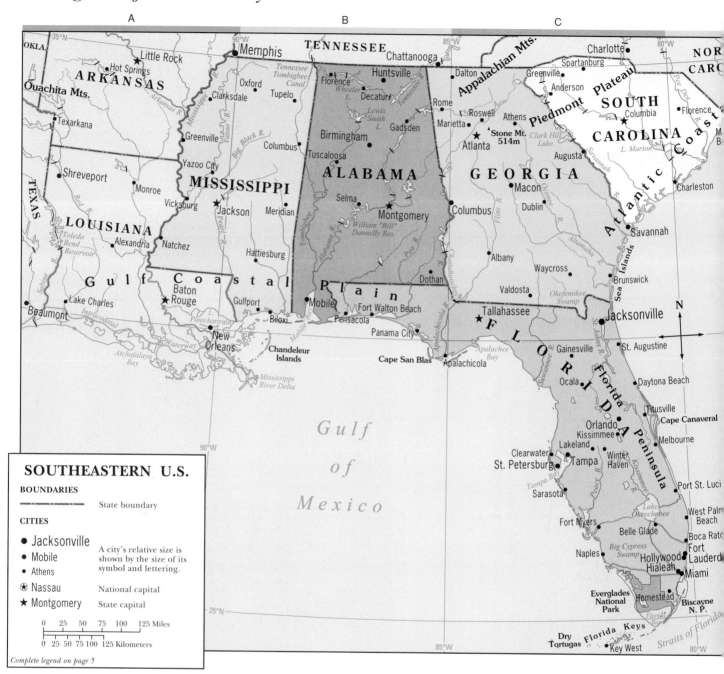

SOUTHEASTERN U.S.

BOUNDARIES

——————————— State boundary

CITIES

● Jacksonville

● Mobile

• Athens

A city's relative size is shown by the size of its symbol and lettering.

⊛ Nassau National capital

★ Montgomery State capital

| 0 | 25 | 50 | 75 | 100 | 125 Miles |
| 0 | 25 | 50 | 75 | 100 | 125 Kilometers |

Complete legend on page 5

In Charleston, South Carolina, old homes feature large, shady porches for enjoying cool breezes.

Miami delights with warm weather, lively colors, and palm trees.

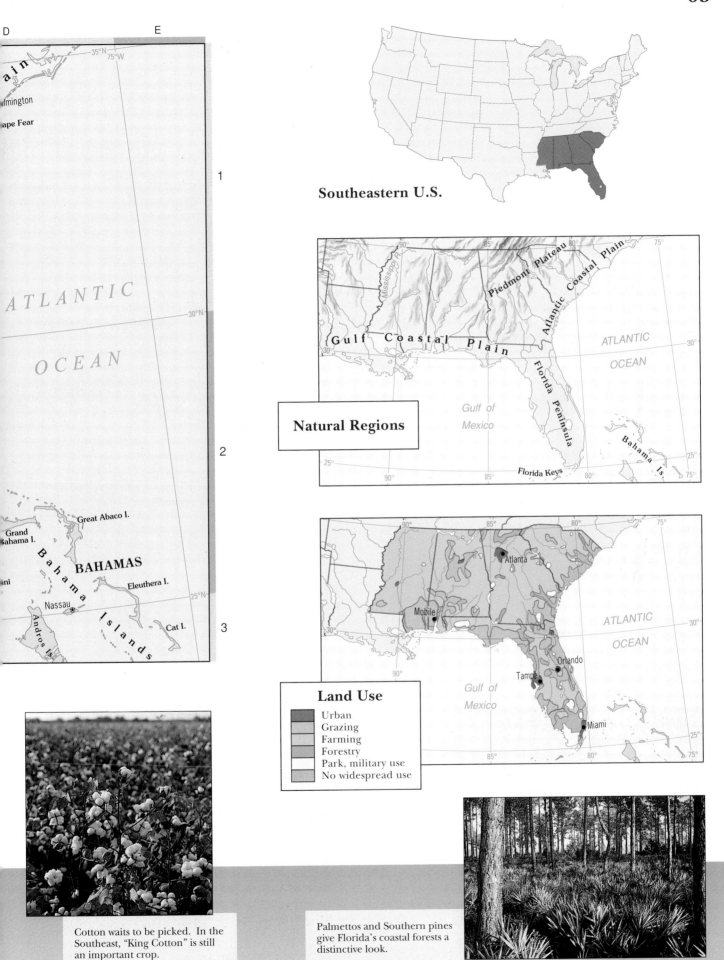

D   E

35°N 75°W

1

Imington

ape Fear

ATLANTIC

30°N

OCEAN

2

Great Abaco I.

Grand
Bahama I.

BAHAMAS

Eleuthera I.

ani

Nassau

25°N

3

Andros Is.

Cat I.

Bahama Islands

Southeastern U.S.

Natural Regions

Piedmont Plateau

Atlantic Coastal Plain

Gulf   Coastal   Plain

Mississippi R.

Florida Peninsula

ATLANTIC

OCEAN

30°

Gulf of
Mexico

Bahama Is.

25°

Florida Keys

Land Use

Atlanta

Mobile

Orlando

Tampa

ATLANTIC

OCEAN

30°

Gulf of
Mexico

Miami

25°

- Urban
- Grazing
- Farming
- Forestry
- Park, military use
- No widespread use

Cotton waits to be picked. In the
Southeast, "King Cotton" is still
an important crop.

Palmettos and Southern pines
give Florida's coastal forests a
distinctive look.

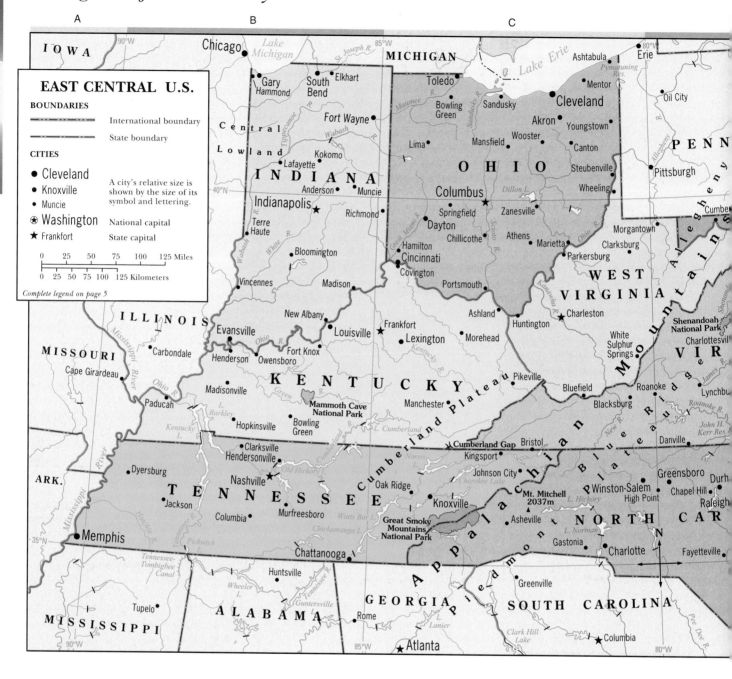

EAST CENTRAL U.S.

BOUNDARIES

━━━━━ International boundary

───── State boundary

CITIES

● Cleveland

● Knoxville

• Muncie

A city's relative size is shown by the size of its symbol and lettering.

✪ Washington   National capital

★ Frankfort   State capital

```
0   25   50   75   100  125 Miles
0  25 50 75 100  125 Kilometers
```

Complete legend on page 5

IOWA · Chicago · MICHIGAN · Lake Michigan · Lake Erie · Ashtabula · Erie · Pymatuning Res. · Oil City · PENN · Gary · Hammond · South Bend · Elkhart · Toledo · Mentor · Cleveland · St. Joseph R. · Bowling Green · Sandusky · Akron · Youngstown · Fort Wayne · Central · Lowland · Maumee R. · Lima · Mansfield · Wooster · Canton · Tippecanoe · Wabash · Kokomo · OHIO · Steubenville · Wheeling · Allegheny R. · Pittsburgh · INDIANA · Lafayette · Anderson · Muncie · Columbus · Dillon L. · Morgantown · Indianapolis · Richmond · Springfield · Zanesville · Clarksburg · Terre Haute · White R. · Dayton · Hamilton · Chillicothe · Athens · Marietta · Parkersburg · WEST · VIRGINIA · Cumbe · Bloomington · Great Miami R. · Cincinnati · Covington · Scioto R. · Ohio R. · Portsmouth · Kanawha R. · Charleston · Shenandoah National Park · Charlottesvil · Vincennes · Madison · New Albany · Ashland · Morehead · White Sulphur Springs · VIR · ILLINOIS · Evansville · Louisville · Frankfort · Lexington · Huntington · Mountains · Blue Ridge · Shen · MISSOURI · Fort Knox · Kentucky R. · KENTUCKY · Cumberland Plateau · Pikeville · Bluefield · Roanoke · James R. · Lynchburg · Cape Girardeau · Henderson · Owensboro · Mississippi River · Ohio R. · Madisonville · Manchester · Blacksburg · Roanoke R. · John H. Kerr Res. · Paducah · L. Barkley · Hopkinsville · Mammoth Cave National Park · Bowling Green · Green R. · L. Cumberland · Cumberland Gap · Bristol · Danville · Kentucky L. · Cumberland R. · Kingsport · Johnson City · Greensboro · ARK. · Dyersburg · Clarksville · Hendersonville · Old Hickory L. · Norris L. · Oak Ridge · Cherokee Lake · Winston-Salem · High Point · Durh · Chapel Hill · Raleigh · Nashville · Mt. Mitchell 2037m · L. Hickory · NORTH · CAR · TENNESSEE · Jackson · Columbia · Murfreesboro · Watts Bar L. · Knoxville · Asheville · L. Norman · Memphis · Mississippi R. · Duck R. · Chickamauga L. · Great Smoky Mountains National Park · Gastonia · Charlotte · Fayetteville · Pickwick L. · Tennessee R. · Chattanooga · Piedmont · Appalachian · Tennessee-Tombigbee Canal · Huntsville · Wheeler L. · Guntersville L. · GEORGIA · SOUTH CAROLINA · Pee Dee R. · Tupelo · ALABAMA · Rome · Greenville · Clark Hill Lake · MISSISSIPPI · L. Lanier · Atlanta · Columbia

Sleek horses graze on Kentucky bluegrass. The grass gets its name from tiny blue flowers that bloom in May.

Farmers, suburban families, and fishermen share Chesapeake Bay. The bay extends 200 miles inland from the Atlantic.

E

NEW YORK

CONN.

Susquehanna R. • Scranton

• Wilkes-Barre

VANIA

Delaware R.

75°W

• Newark

New York

• Allentown

• Trenton

★ Harrisburg

Philadelphia

NEW JERSEY

40°N

• Wilmington

Hagerstown s

Baltimore

• Columbia

• Dover

Delaware Bay

ington D.C.

• Annapolis

Cape May

arlington

• Alexandria

DELAWARE

MARYLAND

• Ocean City

Potomac R.

Chesapeake Bay

Assateague I.

ricksburg

Rappahannock R.

NIA

ATLANTIC

mond

• Williamsburg

• Hampton

Cape Charles

Newport News

• Norfolk

OCEAN

Portsmouth

Virginia Beach

Great Dismal Swamp

Roanoke R.

ton

Kitty Hawk

Rocky Mount

Albemarle Sound

Hatteras I.

• Greenville

Pamlico Sound

Cape Hatteras

NA

• Goldsboro

Neuse R.

35°N

antic

• Jacksonville

Coastal

Cape Lookout

• Wilmington

Cape Fear

75°W

1

2

3

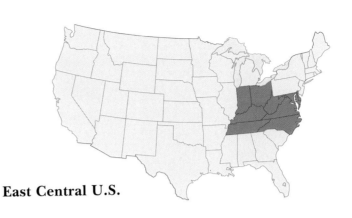

East Central U.S.

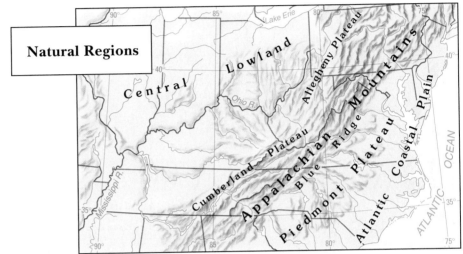

Natural Regions

Central Lowland

Lake Erie

Allegheny Plateau

40°

Ohio R.

Appalachian Mountains

Cumberland Plateau

Blue Ridge

Piedmont Plateau

Atlantic Coastal Plain

35°

ATLANTIC OCEAN

Mississippi R.

75°

90° 85° 80°

Land Use

■	Urban
	Grazing
	Farming
	Forestry
	Park, military use
	No widespread use

Lake Erie

• Cleveland

40°

• Cincinnati

Washington, D.C.

• Norfolk

• Durham

• Nashville

35°

• Charlotte

ATLANTIC OCEAN

90° 85° 80° 75°

Can you see how the Great Smokies got their name? Mist often fills the region's valleys.

The U.S. Capitol and the Washington Monument gleam white against the sky at sunset.

Northeastern U.S.

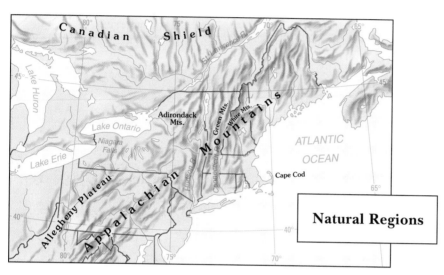

Natural Regions

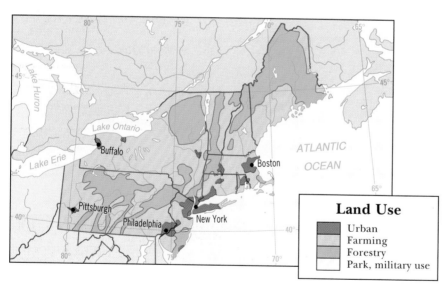

Land Use

- Urban
- Farming
- Forestry
- Park, military use

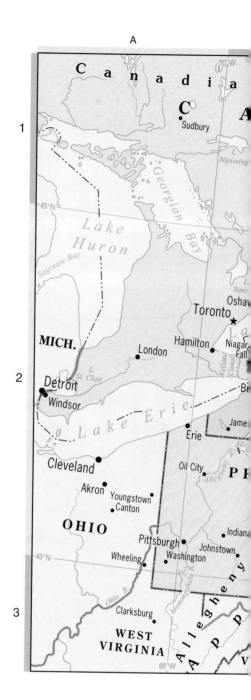

The twin towers of the World Trade Center dominate the skyline of New York City.

The Allegheny River flows past broad-leaf forests in western Pennsylvania. Much of the Northeast remains rural.

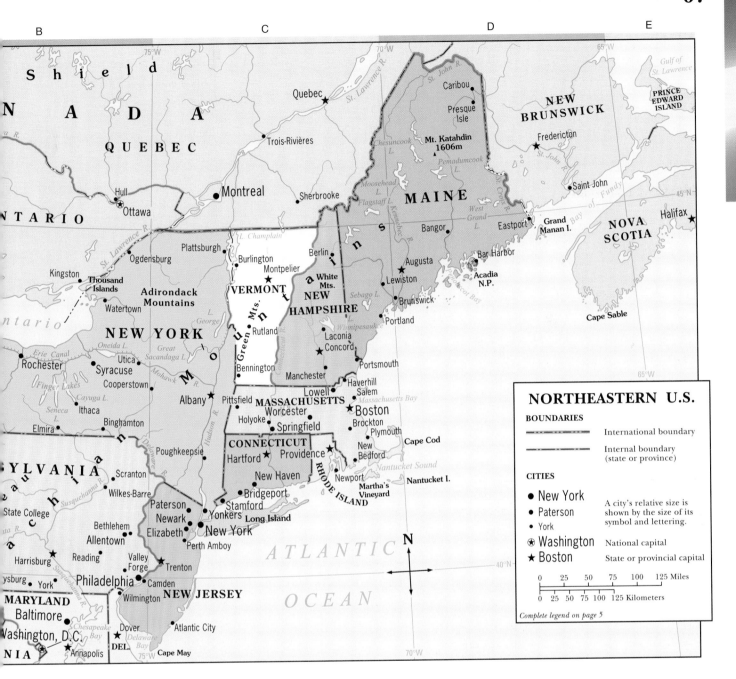

Shield

CANADA

QUEBEC

Quebec

Trois-Rivières

Hull
Ottawa

ONTARIO

Montreal

Sherbrooke

St. Lawrence R.

Caribou

Presque Isle

NEW BRUNSWICK

Fredericton

Saint John

St. John R.

Gulf of St. Lawrence

PRINCE EDWARD ISLAND

MAINE

Mt. Katahdin 1606m

Chesuncook L.

Pemadumcook L.

Moosehead L.

Flagstaff L.

Bangor

Augusta

Lewiston

Brunswick

Portland

Eastport

Grand Manan I.

Bay of Fundy

NOVA SCOTIA

Halifax

Cape Sable

Acadia N.P.

Bar Harbor

Plattsburgh

Ogdensburg

Kingston

Thousand Islands

Watertown

Adirondack Mountains

Burlington

Montpelier

VERMONT

Berlin

White Mts.

NEW HAMPSHIRE

Green Mts.

Sebago L.

L. Champlain

L. George

NEW YORK

Rutland

Bennington

Rochester

Syracuse

Cooperstown

Albany

Pittsfield

Utica

Oneida L.

Erie Canal

Finger Lakes

Cayuga L.

Seneca L.

Ithaca

Elmira

Binghamton

Great Sacandaga L.

Mohawk R.

Laconia

Concord

Manchester

L. Winnipesaukee

Portsmouth

Haverhill

Salem

Lowell

MASSACHUSETTS

Worcester

Holyoke

Springfield

Boston

Brockton

Plymouth

Massachusetts Bay

Cape Cod

CONNECTICUT

Hartford

Providence

New Haven

RHODE ISLAND

New Bedford

Newport

Nantucket Sound

Martha's Vineyard

Nantucket I.

Poughkeepsie

Hudson R.

Delaware R.

SYLVANIA

Appalachian

Scranton

Wilkes-Barre

State College

Bethlehem

Allentown

Reading

Harrisburg

Susquehanna R.

Gettysburg

York

Philadelphia

Camden

Wilmington

Paterson

Newark

Elizabeth

Yonkers

Stamford

Bridgeport

Perth Amboy

New York

Long Island

Valley Forge

Trenton

NEW JERSEY

Atlantic City

Cape May

Dover

DEL.

Delaware Bay

MARYLAND

Baltimore

Washington, D.C.

Annapolis

Chesapeake Bay

NIA

ATLANTIC OCEAN

N

NORTHEASTERN U.S.

BOUNDARIES

International boundary

Internal boundary (state or province)

CITIES

● **New York**

● Paterson

· York

A city's relative size is shown by the size of its symbol and lettering.

⊛ **Washington** National capital

★ **Boston** State or provincial capital

| 0 | 25 | 50 | 75 | 100 | 125 Miles |

| 0 | 25 | 50 | 75 | 100 | 125 Kilometers |

Complete legend on page 5

Near Boston Harbor, history and an amazing variety of food shops attract visitors to Faneuil Hall and Quincy Market.

Boats dry in the sun and sea grass of Cape Cod. The cape is a favorite summertime vacation spot in Massachusetts.

State	Largest City	Capital	Admitted to Union (Order)	U.S. House Members	Population	Rank in Pop.	Percentage Urban
Alabama	Birmingham	Montgomery	1819 (22)	7	4,219,000	22	60%
Alaska	Anchorage	Juneau	1959 (49)	1	606,000	48	67%
Arizona	Phoenix	Phoenix	1912 (48)	6	4,075,000	23	87%
Arkansas	Little Rock	Little Rock	1836 (25)	4	2,453,000	33	53%
California	Los Angeles	Sacramento	1850 (31)	52	31,431,000	1	93%
Colorado	Denver	Denver	1876 (38)	6	3,656,000	26	82%
Connecticut	Bridgeport	Hartford	1788 (5)	6	3,275,000	27	79%
Delaware	Wilmington	Dover	1787 (1)	1	706,000	46	73%
Florida	Jacksonville	Tallahassee	1845 (27)	23	13,953,000	4	85%
Georgia	Atlanta	Atlanta	1788 (4)	11	7,055,000	11	63%
Hawaii	Honolulu	Honolulu	1959 (50)	2	1,179,000	40	89%
Idaho	Boise	Boise	1890 (43)	2	1,133,000	42	57%
Illinois	Chicago	Springfield	1818 (21)	20	11,752,000	6	85%
Indiana	Indianapolis	Indianapolis	1816 (19)	10	5,752,000	14	65%
Iowa	Des Moines	Des Moines	1846 (29)	5	2,829,000	30	61%
Kansas	Wichita	Topeka	1861 (34)	4	2,554,000	32	69%
Kentucky	Louisville	Frankfort	1792 (15)	6	3,827,000	24	52%
Louisiana	New Orleans	Baton Rouge	1812 (18)	7	4,315,000	21	68%
Maine	Portland	Augusta	1820 (23)	2	1,240,000	39	45%
Maryland	Baltimore	Annapolis	1788 (7)	8	5,006,000	19	81%
Massachusetts	Boston	Boston	1788 (6)	10	6,041,000	13	84%
Michigan	Detroit	Lansing	1837 (26)	16	9,496,000	8	70%
Minnesota	Minneapolis	St. Paul	1858 (32)	8	4,567,000	20	70%
Mississippi	Jackson	Jackson	1817 (20)	5	2,669,000	31	47%
Missouri	Kansas City	Jefferson City	1821 (24)	9	5,278,000	16	69%

Postal Abbrev.	State Nickname	State Tree	State Flower	State Bird	Area in Sq. Mi. Sq. Km	Rank in Area
AL	The Heart of Dixie Camellia State	Southern pine (Longleaf pine)	Camelia	Yellowhammer	51,718 133 950	29
AK	The Last Frontier	Sitka spruce	Forget-me-not	Willow ptarmigan	591,004 1 530 693	1
AZ	Grand Canyon State	Paloverde	Saguaro blossom	Cactus wren	114,007 295 276	6
AR	Land of Opportunity	Pine	Apple blossom	Mockingbird	53,183 137 742	27
CA	Golden State	California redwood	Golden poppy	California valley quail	158,648 410 896	3
CO	Centennial State	Colorado blue spruce	Rocky Mountain columbine	Lark bunting	104,100 269 618	8
CT	Constitution State Nutmeg State	White oak	Mountain laurel	Robin	5,006 12 966	48
DE	First State Diamond State	American holly	Peach blossom	Blue hen chicken	2,026 5 246	49
FL	Sunshine State	Sabel palm	Orange blossom	Mockingbird	58,681 151 982	22
GA	Peach State Empire State of the South	Live oak	Cherokee rose	Brown thrasher	58,930 152 627	21
HI	Aloha State	Kukui	Yellow hibiscus	Nene (Hawaiian goose)	6,459 16 729	47
ID	Gem State	Western white pine	Syringa	Mountain bluebird	83,574 216 456	13
IL	Prairie State Land of Lincoln	White oak	Native violet	Cardinal	56,343 145 928	24
IN	Hoosier State	Tulip poplar	Peony	Cardinal	36,185 93 720	38
IA	Hawkeye State	Oak	Wild rose	Eastern goldfinch	56,276 145 754	25
KS	Sunflower State	Cottonwood	Native Sunflower	Western meadowlark	82,282 213 110	14
KY	Bluegrass State	Kentucky coffeetree	Goldenrod	Cardinal	40,411 104 665	37
LA	Pelican State	Bald cypress	Magnolia	Brown pelican	47,720 123 593	31
ME	Pine Tree State	White pine	White pine cone and tassel	Chickadee	33,128 85 801	39
MD	Old Line State Free State	White oak (Wye oak)	Black-eyed Susan	Baltimore oriole	10,455 27 077	42
MA	Bay State Old Colony	American elm	Mayflower	Chickadee	8,262 21 398	45
MI	Wolverine State Great Lakes State	White pine	Apple blossom	Robin	58,513 151 548	23
MN	Gopher State North Star State	Norway pine (Red pine)	Pink and white lady's-slipper	Common loon	84,397 218 587	12
MS	Magnolia State	Magnolia	Magnolia	Mockingbird	47,695 123 530	32
MO	Show Me State	Flowering dogwood	Hawthorn	Bluebird	69,709 180 546	19

State	Largest City	Capital	Admitted to Union (Order)	U.S. House Members	Population	Rank in Pop.	Percentage Urban
Montana	Billings	Helena	1889 (41)	1	856,000	44	52%
Nebraska	Omaha	Lincoln	1867 (37)	3	1,623,000	37	66%
Nevada	Las Vegas	Carson City	1864 (36)	2	1,457,000	38	88%
New Hampshire	Manchester	Concord	1788 (9)	2	1,137,000	41	51%
New Jersey	Newark	Trenton	1787 (3)	13	7,904,000	9	89%
New Mexico	Albuquerque	Santa Fe	1912 (47)	3	1,654,000	36	73%
New York	New York City	Albany	1788 (11)	31	18,169,000	3	84%
North Carolina	Charlotte	Raleigh	1789 (12)	12	7,070,000	10	50%
North Dakota	Fargo	Bismarck	1889 (39)	1	638,000	47	53%
Ohio	Columbus	Columbus	1803 (17)	19	11,102,000	7	74%
Oklahoma	Oklahoma City	Oklahoma City	1907 (46)	6	3,258,000	28	68%
Oregon	Portland	Salem	1859 (33)	5	3,086,000	29	70%
Pennsylvania	Philadelphia	Harrisburg	1787 (2)	21	12,052,000	5	69%
Rhode Island	Providence	Providence	1790 (13)	2	997,000	43	86%
South Carolina	Columbia	Columbia	1788 (8)	6	3,664,000	25	55%
South Dakota	Sioux Falls	Pierre	1889 (40)	1	721,000	45	50%
Tennessee	Memphis	Nashville	1796 (16)	9	5,175,000	17	61%
Texas	Houston	Austin	1845 (28)	30	18,378,000	2	80%
Utah	Salt Lake City	Salt Lake City	1896 (45)	3	1,908,000	34	87%
Vermont	Burlington	Montpelier	1791 (14)	1	580,000	49	32%
Virginia	Virginia Beach	Richmond	1788 (10)	11	6,552,000	12	69%
Washington	Seattle	Olympia	1889 (42)	9	5,343,000	15	76%
West Virginia	Charleston	Charleston	1863 (35)	3	1,822,000	35	36%
Wisconsin	Milwaukee	Madison	1848 (30)	9	5,082,000	18	66%
Wyoming	Cheyenne	Cheyenne	1890 (44)	1	476,000	50	65%

Postal Abbrev.	State Nickname	State Tree	State Flower	State Bird	Area in Sq. Mi. Sq. Km	Rank in Area
MT	Treasure State	Ponderosa pine	Bitterroot	Western meadowlark	147,047 380 849	4
NE	Cornhusker State	Cottonwood	Goldenrod	Western meadowlark	77,359 200 358	15
NV	Silver State Sagebrush State	Single-leaf piñon and bristle-cone pine	Sagebrush	Mountain bluebird	110,567 286 367	7
NH	Granite State	White birch	Purple lilac	Purple finch	9,283 24 044	44
NJ	Garden State	Red oak	Purple violet	Eastern goldfinch	7,790 20 175	46
NM	Land of Enchantment	Piñon (Nut pine)	Yucca flower	Roadrunner	121,599 314 939	5
NY	Empire State	Sugar maple	Rose	Bluebird	49,112 127 200	30
NC	Tar Heel State Old North State	Longleaf pine	Flowering dogwood	Cardinal	52,672 136 421	28
ND	Flickertail State Peace Garden State	American elm	Wild prairie rose	Western meadowlark	70,704 183 123	17
OH	Buckeye State	Buckeye	Red carnation	Cardinal	41,328 107 040	35
OK	Sooner State	Redbud	Mistletoe	Scissor-tailed flycatcher	69,903 181 048	18
OR	Beaver State	Douglas fir	Oregon grape	Western meadowlark	97,052 251 365	10
PA	Keystone State	Hemlock	Mountain laurel	Ruffed grouse	45,310 117 351	33
RI	Ocean State Little Rhody	Red maple	Violet	Rhode Island Red	1,213 3 142	50
SC	Palmetto State	Palmetto	Carolina jessamine	Carolina wren	31,117 80 593	40
SD	Mount Rushmore State Coyote State	Black Hills spruce	American pasqueflower	Chinese ring-necked pheasant	77,122 199 744	16
TN	Volunteer State	Tulip poplar	Iris	Mockingbird	42,146 109 158	34
TX	Lone Star State	Pecan	Bluebonnet	Mockingbird	266,874 691 201	2
UT	Beehive State	Blue spruce	Sego lily	Seagull	84,905 219 902	11
VT	Green Mountain State	Sugar maple	Red clover	Hermit thrush	9,615 24 903	43
VA	Old Dominion	Dogwood	Dogwood	Cardinal	40,598 105 149	36
WA	Evergreen State	Western hemlock	Coast rhododendron	Willow goldfinch	68,126 176 446	20
WV	Mountain State	Sugar maple	Rhododendron	Cardinal	24,231 62 759	41
WI	Badger State	Sugar maple	Wood violet	Robin	56,145 145 414	26
WY	Equality State	Cottonwood	Indian paintbrush	Meadowlark	97,818 253 349	9

The index lists place names that appear on the maps and briefly describes where or what they are. Besides page numbers, it also uses a map code for location. The map code refers to the letters and numbers that border each map and divide it into sections. The letter-number code for a place identifies the section of the map where it can be found.

The entry for a physical feature is alphabetized by the proper part of its name, not by the descriptive part. For example, Lake Superior is listed as *Superior, L.,* and Mount McKinley is listed as *McKinley, Mt.* The entry for a city, however, is alphabetized by the first word in its name, no matter what it is. For examples, the city of Lake Charles, Louisiana, is listed as *Lake Charles.* Similarly, foreign names such as Rio Grande are alphabetized by the first word in the name.

Names beginning with *St.* are spelled *Saint* in the index. Abbreviations that are used in the index and in other parts of the book are listed inside the back cover.